TEACHING OUTDOOR CREATIVELY

Teaching Outdoors Creatively offers guidance and a variety of exciting ideas to suit the full range of primary schools and locations. Underpinned by current research and practical experience, it investigates innovative approaches to working creatively with children beyond the classroom.

While recognising the diverse needs and opportunities that primary schools have to develop the outdoors as part of their curriculum, it presents a broad range of activities, philosophies and approaches. Key themes explored include:

- Understanding and using local and home environments
- Investigating streets and buildings in your area
- Planning fieldwork
- Using rivers to inspire children
- Forest schools
- Beach schools
- Physical education outdoors
- Learning through adventure.

Teaching Outdoors Creatively supports teaching and learning in a wide range of settings, from schools in rural and urban areas, to off-site outdoor education centres and residential visits. With a focus on developing effective and stimulating learning environments for children it is a must-have resource for all busy trainee and practising teachers.

Stephen Pickering is Course Leader for Primary and Outdoor Education and Senior Lecturer in Education at the University of Worcester, UK.

THE LEARNING TO TEACH IN THE PRIMARY SCHOOL SERIES

Series editor: Teresa Cremin, The Open University, UK

Teaching is an art form. It demands not only knowledge and understanding of the core areas of learning, but also the ability to teach these creatively and foster learner creativity in the process. The *Learning to Teach in the Primary School* series draws upon recent research which indicates the rich potential of creative teaching and learning, and explores what it means to teach creatively in the primary phase. It also responds to the evolving nature of subject teaching in a wider, more imaginatively framed twenty-first-century primary curriculum.

Designed to complement the textbook *Learning to Teach in the Primary School*, the well informed, lively texts in this series offer support for students and practising teachers who want to develop more creative approaches to teaching and learning. Uniquely, the books highlight the importance of the teachers' own creative engagement and share a wealth of research-informed ideas to enrich pedagogy and practice.

Titles in the series:

TEACHING OUTDOORS CREATIVELY

Edited by
Stephen Pickering

Routledge
Taylor & Francis Group

LONDON AND NEW YORK

First published 2017
by Routledge
2 Park Square, Milton Park, Abingdon, Oxon OX14 4RN

and by Routledge
711 Third Avenue, New York, NY 10017

Routledge is an imprint of the Taylor & Francis Group, an informa business

British Library Cataloguing in Publication Data
A catalogue record for this book is available from the British Library

Library of Congress Cataloging in Publication Data
Names: Pickering, Stephen, 1965–
Title: Teaching outdoors creatively / edited by Stephen Pickering.
Description: New York : Routledge, 2017.
Identifiers: LCCN 2016048029 | ISBN 9781138642379 (hardback) |
ISBN 9781138642386 (pbk.) | ISBN 9781315630021 (electronic)
Subjects: LCSH: Outdoor education. | Experiential learning.
Classification: LCC LB1047 .T43 2017 | DDC 371.3/84—dc23
LC record available at https://lccn.loc.gov/2016048029

ISBN: 978-1-138-64237-9 (hbk)
ISBN: 978-1-138-64238-6 (pbk)
ISBN: 978-1-315-63002-1 (ebk)

Typeset in Times New Roman and Helvetica Neue
by Florence Production Ltd, Stoodleigh, Devon

CONTENTS

CONTENTS ■ ■ ■ ■

CONTRIBUTORS

Sara Knight is a retired academic from Anglia Ruskin University and a Forest School leader. She has contributed to the development Forest School in the UK, publishing academic papers and text books on this subject, and has been a keynote speaker at conferences in the UK, Europe, Asia and Canada.

Margaret Mackintosh was a primary teacher in Humberside then Senior Lecturer in Primary Geography Education at Plymouth University. She is a member of the Geographical Association's Early Years and Primary Phase committee and serves on the editorial board of *Primary Geography*, for which she was Honorary Editor. Her particular interests are visual literacy and linking art and geography.

Paula Owens has a range of primary classroom experience as a class teacher, subject leader, deputy and head teacher. She has worked in Initial Teacher Education and was curriculum development leader at the Geographical Association for many years. Paula is currently an independent education advisor. She is consultant to the Geographical Association and a member of both their Early Years and Primary Phase Committee and the Primary Geography Editorial Board. Paula is a Geography Champion and a member of the Geography Expert Subject Advisory Group (GESAG).

Stephen Pickering is Course Leader for Primary and Outdoor Education at the University of Worcester and Senior Lecturer in Primary Education. He is a Forest School Leader and a consultant for the Geographical Association (GA) where he sits on the GA's Primary Geography editorial board. Stephen has written chapters for *Learning to Teach in the Primary School*, and *Teaching Geography Creatively*, both books in this series.

Lee Pritchard is Course Leader for the Outdoor Adventure Leadership and Management degree programme at the University of Worcester. He is a qualified secondary school teacher and has been involved extensively in the outdoor adventure education industry both in the UK and overseas. He is, amongst other things, a Mountaineering Instructor, Level 4 Kayak coach and Forest School practitioner. His current work involves delivering on a range of mountain training awards, leading schools expeditions overseas, climbing in the French Alps and winter mountaineering in the Scottish mountains.

Stephen Scoffham is Visiting Reader in Sustainability and Education at Canterbury Christ Church University, UK. A leading member of the Geographical Association, he began his career as a primary school teacher before becoming schools' officer at an Urban Studies Centre. In addition to serving as a schools' atlas consultant, Stephen is also the author of many articles, books and resources on primary geography. He is the editor of *Teaching Geography Creatively*, which won the Geographical Association gold award in 2014 and is part of the series to which this book belongs.

Julia Tanner is a former teacher and teacher educator, now working as an education consultant, trainer and author. She is passionate about promoting outdoor learning for the benefits it offers children and teachers. Julia has a long-standing interest in children's wellbeing, and in how primary schools can provide an environment and curriculum which nurtures their holistic development. She is a member of the Geographical Association's Early Years and Primary Phase Committee and its Publishing Board, and the editor of the Everyday Guide to Primary Geography Series.

Jane Whittle is the IB PYP Coordinator at the International School of Como, Italy. She is a member of the *Primary Geography* Editorial Board, a Geography Champion for the Geographical Association and an IB MYP Examiner for Geography. She is co-author of a number of texts including *Back2Front: The Americas* and *The Everyday Guide to Teaching Geography: Story*.

Sarah Williams taught in primary, secondary and special schools in New Zealand and the North of England before joining Sheffield Hallam University four years ago as a Primary and Early Years PE Specialist. She currently leads a PGCE Primary PE specialist programme within the Sheffield Institute of Education. Sarah's main areas of interest and research focus on the development of fundamental skills and integrated physical activity programmes.

Sharon Witt is Senior Lecturer in Education at the University of Winchester. Her research interests include playful, experiential approaches to primary geography and outdoor learning. With a colleague, she is currently exploring teaching and learning ideas that connect children to environments through place attention and responsiveness (@Attention2place). Sharon is studying for a professional doctorate at the University of Exeter.

Colin Wood is a Senior Lecturer in Outdoor Education at the University of Worcester. He had a long career in outdoor education in the UK and overseas. He now teaches and writes about outdoor learning.

SERIES EDITOR'S FOREWORD

Teresa Cremin

Over recent decades teachers working in accountability cultures across the globe have been required to focus on raising standards, setting targets, and 'delivering' prescribed curricula and pedagogy. The language of schooling, Mottram and Hall (2009: 109) assert, has predominantly focused on 'oversimplified, easily measurable notions of attainment' which, they argue, has had a homogenising effect, prompting children and their development to be discussed 'according to levels and descriptors', rather than as children and unique learners. Practitioners, positioned as passive recipients of the prescribed agenda, appear to have had their hands tied, their voices quietened and their professional autonomy both threatened and constrained. At times, the relentless quest for higher standards has obscured the personal and affective dimensions of teaching and learning, fostering a mindset characterised more by compliance and conformity than curiosity and creativity.

However, in many countries efforts have been made to re-ignite teachers' and learners' creativity, since it is seen to be essential to economic and cultural development, as well as personally enhancing. In the UK, the recent impetus for creativity in education can be traced back to the National Advisory Committee on Creative and Cultural Education (NACCCE, 1999), which recommended a core role for creativity in teaching and learning. Primary schools in England were encouraged to explore ways to offer more innovative and creative curricula (DfES, 2003) and new national curricula in Scotland also foregrounded children's critical and creative thinking. Additionally, initiatives such as Creative Partnerships, an English government-funded initiative to nurture children's creativity, inspired some teachers to reconstruct their pedagogy (Galton, 2010). Many other schools and teachers, encouraged by these initiatives, and determined to offer creative and engaging school experiences, have exercised the 'power to innovate' (Lance, 2006). Some have proactively sought ways to shape the curriculum responsively, appropriating national policies in their own contexts and showing professional commitment and imagination, despite, or perhaps because of, the persistent performative agenda (e.g. Cremin et al., 2015; Neelands, 2009; Jeffrey and Woods, 2009).

Schools continue to be exhorted to be more innovative in curriculum construction and national curricula afford opportunities for all teachers to seize the space, exert their professionalism and shape their own curricula in collaboration with the young people with whom they are working. Yet for primary educators, tensions persist, not only because the dual policies of performativity and creativity appear contradictory, but also perhaps because teachers' own confidence as creative educators, indeed as creative individuals, has been radically reduced by the constant barrage of change and challenge. As Csikszentmihalyi (2011) notes, teachers lack a theoretically underpinned framework for creativity that can be developed in practice; they need support to develop as artistically engaged, research-informed curriculum co-developers. Eisner (2003) asserts that teaching is an art form, whilst Sawyer (2011) describes it as an 'act of improvisation' and argues that teachers benefit from viewing themselves as versatile artists in the classroom, drawing on their personal passions and creativity as they teach creatively. The potency of the personal in education and the creativity of the teacher deserve increased attention and development.

As Joubert too observes:

> Creative teaching is an art. One cannot teach teachers didactically how to be creative; there is no failsafe recipe or routine. Some strategies may help to promote creative thinking, but teachers need to develop a full repertoire of skills which they can adapt to different situations.
>
> (Joubert, 2001: 21)

Creative teaching is only part of the picture however, since teaching for creativity also needs to be acknowledged and their mutual dependency recognised. The former focuses more on teachers using imaginative approaches in the classroom (and beyond) in order to make learning more interesting and effective, the latter, more on the development of children's creativity (NACCCE, 1999). In combining these terms Dezuanni and Jetnikoff (2011: 265) assert that creative pedagogies involve 'imaginative and innovative arrangement of curricula and teaching strategies in school classrooms' planned and enacted in order to develop children's creativity. Both rely upon an understanding of the notion of creativity and demand that professionals confront the myths and mantras which surround the word. These include the commonly held misconceptions that creativity is the preserve of the arts or arts education, and that it is confined to particularly gifted individuals.

Creativity, an elusive concept, has been multiply defined by educationalists, psychologists and neurologists, as well as by policy makers in different countries and researchers in different cultural contexts (Glăveanu et al., 2017). Debates resound about its individual and/or collaborative nature, the degree to which it is generic and/or domain-specific, and the differences between the 'Big C' creativity of genius and the 'little c' creativity of the everyday. Notwithstanding these issues, most scholars in the field believe it involves the capacity to generate, to reason and to critically evaluate novel ideas and/or imaginary scenarios. As such, it encompasses thinking through and solving problems, making connections, inventing and reinventing, and flexing one's imaginative muscles in all aspects of learning and life.

In the primary classroom, creative teaching and learning have long been associated with innovation, originality, ownership and control (Woods and Jeffrey, 1996; Jeffrey, 2006) and creative teachers have been seen, in their planning and teaching, and in the ethos which they create, to afford high value to curiosity and risk taking, to ownership, autonomy and making connections (Craft et al., 2014; Cremin et al., 2009; Cremin, 2015, 2017). Such teachers often work in partnership with others: with children, other teachers and experts from beyond the school gates (Cochrane and Cockett, 2007; Davies et al., 2012; Thomson et al., 2012). These partnerships offer new possibilities, with teachers acquiring some of the repertoire of pedagogic practices – the 'signature pedagogies' that artists use (Thomson and Hall, 2015).

Additionally, in research exploring possibility thinking, which Craft (2000) argues drives creativity in education, an intriguing interplay between teachers and children has been observed. In this body of work, with data collected mainly through observations and interviews, children and teachers were seen to immerse themselves in playful contexts, posing questions, being imaginative, showing self-determination, taking risks and innovating – together (Burnard et al., 2006; Cremin et al., 2006; Chappell et al., 2008; Craft et al., 2012; Cremin et al., 2013). As McWilliam (2009) argues, teachers can choose not to position themselves as the all-knowing 'sage on the stage', or the facilitator-like 'guide on the side'. They can choose, as creative practitioners do, to take up a role of the 'meddler in the middle', co-creating curricula in innovative and responsive ways that harness their own and foster the children's creativity. A new pedagogy of possibility beckons.

This series, *Learning to Teach in the Primary School*, which accompanies and complements the edited textbook *Learning to Teach in the Primary School* (Cremin and Burnett, 4th edition, forthcoming), seeks to support teachers in developing as creative practitioners and exploring the synergies between teaching creatively and teaching for creativity. The series does not merely offer practical strategies for use in the classroom, although these abound, but more importantly it seeks to widen teachers' and student teachers' knowledge and understanding of the principles underpinning creative approaches, principles based on research. It seeks to mediate the wealth of research evidence and make accessible and engaging the diverse theoretical perspectives and scholarly arguments available, demonstrating their practical relevance and value to the profession.

Those teachers who aspire to develop further as creative and curious educators will find much of value in the series to support their own professional learning journeys and markedly enrich their pedagogy and practice right across the curriculum.

TERESA CREMIN

Teresa Cremin (Grainger) is a Professor of Education (Literacy) at the Open University and a past President of UKRA (2001–2) and UKLA (2007–9). She is a Fellow of the Royal Society of the Arts (RSA) and of the English Association and the Academy of Social Sciences. Teresa is also currently co-convenor of the BERA Creativity SIG and a Trustee of UKLA. Her work involves research, publication and consultancy in literacy and creativity.

Many of Teresa's current projects seek to explore the nature and characteristics of creative pedagogies, including for example examining immersive theatre and related teaching techniques, children's make-believe play in the context of storytelling and story acting, their everyday lives and literacy practices, and the nature of literary discussions in extracurricular reading groups. Additionally, Teresa is researching creative science practice with learners aged 3–8 years and possibility thinking as a driver for creative learning. Teresa is also passionate about (and still researching) teachers' own creative development and their identity positioning in the classroom as readers, writers, and creative human beings.

Teresa has written and edited over 28 books and numerous papers and professional texts, most recently editing with colleagues *Storytelling in Early Childhood: Language, literacy, and culture* (2017, Routledge); *Writer Identity and the Teaching and Learning of Writing* (2017, Routledge); *Creativity and Creative Pedagogies in the Early and Primary Years* (2017, Routledge); *Researching Literacy Lives*: *Building home-school communities* (2015, Routledge); *Teaching English Creatively* (2nd edition, 2015, Routledge); *Building Communities of Engaged Readers: Reading for pleasure* (2014, Routledge); and *The International Handbook of Research into Children's Literacy, Learning and Culture* (2013, Blackwell).

In addition her book publications since 2000 include: *Writing Voices: Creating communities of writers* (2012, Routledge); *Learning to Teach in the Primary School* (2014, Routledge); *Teaching Writing Effectively*: *Reviewing practice* (2011, UKLA); *Drama, Reading and Writing: Talking our way forwards (*2009, UKLA*); Jumpstart Drama* (2009, David Fulton); *Creative Teaching for Tomorrow: Fostering a creative state of mind* (2009, Future Creative); *Documenting Creative Learning 5–11* (2007, Trentham); *Creativity and Writing: Developing voice and verve* (2005, Routledge);*Teaching English in Higher Education* (2007, NATE and UKLA); *Creative Activities for Character, Setting and Plot, 5–7, 7–9, 9–11* (2004, Scholastic); and *Language and Literacy: A Routledge reader* (2001, Routledge).

REFERENCES

Burnard, P., Craft, A. and Cremin, T. (2006) 'Possibility thinking', *International Journal of Early Years Education,* 14(3): 243–262.

Chappell, K., Craft, A., Burnard, P. and Cremin, T. (2008) Question-posing and Question-responding: the heart of possibility thinking in the early years, *Early Years*, 28(3): 267–286.

Cochrane, P. and Cockett, M. (2007) *Building a Creative School. A dynamic approach to school improvement.* Stoke on Trent, Trentham Books.

Craft, A. (2000) *Creativity Across the Primary Curriculum.* London: Routledge.

Craft, A., Cremin, T., Burnard, P., Dragovic, T. and Chappell, K. (2012) Possibility thinking: culminative studies of an evidence-based concept driving creativity? *Education 3–13*: *International Journal of Primary, Elementary and Early Education,* 41(5): 538–556.

Craft, A., Cremin, T., Hay, P. and Clack, J. (2014) Creative Primary Schools: developing and maintaining pedagogy for creativity, *Ethnography and Education* 9 (1): 16–34.

Cremin, T. (2015) Creative teachers and creative teaching, in A. Wilson (ed.) *Creativity in Primary Education.* London: Sage, pp. 33–44.

Cremin, T. (2017) (ed.) *Creativity and Creative Pedagogies in the Early and Primary Years.* London: Routledge.

Cremin, T. and Arthur, J. (2014) (eds) *Learning to Teach in the Primary School* (3rd edition). London: Routledge.

Cremin, T., Burnard, P. and Craft, A. (2006) Pedagogy and possibility thinking in the early years, *International Journal of Thinking Skills and Creativity*, 1(2): 108–19.

Cremin, T., Barnes, J. and Scoffham, S. (2009) *Creative Teaching for Tomorrow: Fostering a creative state of mind.* Deal: Future Creative.

Cremin, T., Chappell, K. and Craft, A. (2013) Reciprocity between narrative, questioning and imagination in the early and primary years: examining the role of narrative in possibility thinking, *Thinking Skills and Creativity,* 9: 136–151.

Cremin, T. Glauert, E., Craft, A., Compton, A. and Stylianidou, F. (2015) Creative Little Scientists: Exploring pedagogical synergies between inquiry-based and creative approaches in Early Years science, *Education 3–13, International Journal of Primary, Elementary and Early Years Education*, Special issue on creative pedagogies.

Csikszentmihalyi, M. (2011) A systems perspective on creativity and its implications for measurement, in R. Schenkel and O. Quintin (eds), *Measuring Creativity,* 407–414, The European Commission: Brussels.

Davies, D., Jindal-Snape, D., Collier, C., Digby, R., Hay, P. and Howe, A. (2012) Creative learning environments in education. *Thinking Skills and Creativity.* http://dx.doi.org/10.1016/j.tsc.2012.07.004.

Department for Education and Skills (DfES) (2003) *Excellence and Enjoyment: A strategy for primary schools.* Nottingham: DfES.

Department for Culture, Media and Sport (2006). *Government Response to Paul Roberts' Report on Nurturing Creativity in Young People.* London: DCMS

Dezuanni, M. and Jetnikoff, A. (2011) Creative pedagogies and the contemporary school classroom, in J. Sefton Green, P. Thomson, K. Jones, and L. Bresler. *The Routledge International Handbook of Creative Learning.* London: Routledge, pp. 264–272.

Eisner, E. (2003) Artistry in education, *Scandinavian Journal of Educational Research*, 47(3): 373–384.

Galton, M. (2010) Going with the flow or back to normal? The impact of creative practitioners in schools and classrooms, *Research Papers in Education* 25(4): 355–375.

Glăveanu, V., Sierra, Z. and Tanggaard, L. (2017) Widening our understanding of creative pedagogy: A North–South dialogue, in Cremin, T. (2017) (ed.) *Creativity and Creative Pedagogies in the Early and Primary Years*, pp. 1–11. (London: Routledge).

Jeffrey, B. and Woods, P. (2009) *Creative Learning in the Primary School*. London: Routledge.

Jeffrey, B. (ed.) (2006) *Creative Learning Practices: European experiences*. London: Tufnell Press.

Joubert, M. M. (2001) The art of creative teaching: NACCCE and beyond, in A.

Craft, B. Jeffrey and M. Liebling (eds) *Creativity in Education*. London: Continuum.

Lance, A. (2006) Power to innovate? A study of how primary practitioners are negotiating the modernisation agenda, *Ethnography and Education*, 1(3): 333–344.

Mottram, M. and Hall, C. (2009) Diversions and diversity: does the personalisation agenda offer real opportunities for taking children's home literacies seriously?, *English in Education*, 43(2): 98–112.

National Advisory Committee on Creative and Cultural Education (NACCCE) (1999) *All Our Futures: Creativity, culture and education*. London: Department for Education and Employment.

Neelands, J. (2009) Acting together: Ensemble as a democratic process in art and life, *Research in Drama Education*, 14(2): 173–189.

Sawyer, K. (2011) (ed.) *Structure and improvisation in creative teaching*. New York, Cambridge University Press.

Thomson, P., Hall, C., Jones, K. and Sefton-Green, J. (2012) *The Signature Pedagogies Project: Final report*. London: Creativity, Culture and Education. http://www.creativetallis.com/uploads/2/2/8/7/2287089/signature_pedagogies_report_final_version_11.3.12.pdf (1 June 2012).

Thomson, P. and Hall, C. (2015) 'Everyone can imagine their own Gellert': the democratic artist and 'inclusion' in primary and nursery classrooms *Education 3–13: International Journal of Primary, Elementary and Early Years Education*, Special issue on creative pedagogies.

Woods, P. and Jeffrey, B. (1996) *Teachable Moments: The art of creative teaching in primary schools*. Buckingham: Open University Press.

EVERYDAY PLACES AND SPACES

Stephen Pickering

INTRODUCTION

This chapter explores what creative outdoor learning means and relates activities to children discovering place and space in their local area and home environments.

PLACE

As a child at school my everyday place was at my desk, looking out of the window with longing and a sense of resignation. Outdoors was something that happened at 'playtime', whilst learning was restricted to the classroom. But as soon as I was 'let out' of the classroom's four walls I would run, along with all the other children, straight outside, and I would really start to learn. I learned about risk management by clambering over the school fence to play football in the beautiful, yet barricaded, field when the caretaker wasn't watching. I learned about nature and science and English and geography. I built things in the garden and school field and at weekends I learned about independence with a Red Bus Rover ticket that would open up the whole of London by bus and tube. I learned about myself and I gained knowledge . . . everywhere!

Things have moved on greatly since those days and many children engage in regular, school-based learning beyond the classroom walls. Forest Schools, welly Wednesdays, Earth Education, Learn Outside; call it what you will, it is clear that 'learning outside the classroom is important' (House of Commons Children, Schools and Families Committee 2010, p. 3). However, this is a potentially narrow view. Learning creatively outdoors is not restricted to lessons that happen to take place in the school grounds. It is not restricted to field trips, excursions and residential experiences. In fact, controversial as it may seem, learning creatively outdoors does not only have to take place outdoors! Creativity is a notion, I believe, that is rooted in imagination. And with imagination a child can sit at their desk and be anywhere. I have often sat as a child with a book and been transported to the deep woods of Canada or the wild rivers of Nepal, or even my own local woods – in medieval times. But remember that imagination needs feeding, and being outdoors, like reading books, is a great source for firing imaginations. Additionally, part of the love of the outdoors involves stepping from one area to the other, from inside to the fresh experiences that you breathe as you head out, and then later coming back inside afterwards

1

to warm toes and chat about all that happened. Teaching creatively outdoors involves teaching creatively indoors too. There is no exclusivity here.

Schools tend to structure outdoor learning, indeed just about all learning, around an age-based framework (unless of course school numbers encourage mixed age classes). Recent research in Australia has found that mixed age grouping helps children develop social, cognitive and language skills, with children engaging in 'more mature and complex play' (Rouse, 2015, p. 743). Children will naturally mix with children of different age groups at 'playtime' outside on the school field or playground. Perhaps it is worth challenging the notion that learning outdoors is based on a structure whereby a class is simply taken outside, but where a school supports the social and cognitive opportunities of mixing classes and age groups to learn in a wide range of environments. Should Forest School be restricted to your school's Year One class? Why not take a mix of classes with some pupils from each year? Perhaps our outdoor experiences as teachers can be the foundation to challenge many accepted notions of what education should look like.

SPACE

The outdoor environment provides space. Space has different contexts and nuances which can impact on children physically, psychologically and socially. We have such a wonderfully wide variety of primary schools and primary school settings that we must also surely have a wonderfully broad range of outdoor settings: from woodlands to concrete yards, from small spaces just beyond the doors to expanses of land (or water) that stretch away as far as a child can see. I have taught in a school where the children could sometimes watch deer coming out of the woods on to the school field and I have also taught in a school where, in whichever direction I looked, I was unable to see a tree. Clearly some outdoor areas provide a better range of learning experiences than others, but to a large extent it is not the actual place that matters so much as the meanings, experiences and thoughts that a child attaches to those places. Their notion of space may be very different to ours. Have you ever returned to the school you went to as a child and found the smell instantly memorable but the space just wrong? Too tiny? To provide an easy example, what may appear to be a dusty old bush at the far end of the playground to an adult may be a castle or an escape or a magical forest to a child.

THE SOCIAL LEARNING SCHOOL OF THOUGHT

For many communities of both children and families the growth of digital technology has heralded a change in the social nature of learning (Gray and MacBlain, 2015). This is not to imply that all children go home and sit in front of some form of screen, but nevertheless the social nature of learning and engagement outside school has changed. Children can chat to each other from the comfort of their sofa through social media, and their perspectives on the world have been broadened far beyond their local environment through the internet. The interactive games playing out on the screens in front of our children are the new storytellers. There is a theory that the different societal structures between Northern and Southern European countries today, with young people from Northern countries spending far more time in front of screens than their Southern counterparts, may actually stem from how societies adapted to our differing climates. In Northern countries the fireplace developed as the focus to a home and storytelling was a key element of family and community life. Northern European countries have a strong and ancient storytelling tradition. In Southern Europe the people could live day to day outside for far longer and food was plentiful therefore cooking and the dinner table became the social core for families and communities. Whilst in Southern Europe the tradition of the kitchen table filled with sumptuous Mediterranean cooking has largely remained and continues to shape family and community life, the Northern fireplace and storytelling traditions have largely been replaced by central heating and television. Nevertheless, storytelling remains integral to our society and those who have taken a group of children out to sit on logs round a fire and listen and tell stories will realise the bonding effect of stories told within and about our own environments. Bandura (1977, 1997) developed the theories of the social learning school of thought beyond its behaviourist roots, proposing that social factors, combined with the motivation to join in, together with observed learning, were key factors in a child's development and learning. Compare for a moment the aspects of motivation that may be created by engaging in imaginary play from an interactive games console to that of a Forest School. They both involve discovery, trying new things, managing success and failure, and often, but not always, interaction with others either directly or indirectly. Yes, they are hugely different experientially, but in some ways they are not too dissimilar. Could it be that the teenage games station aficionado is in fact forming a bridge between the social aspects of learning he developed in a Forest School as a young child, to re-engagement with the outside world when he finally rises from the sofa as a young adult and steps outside again? My argument is that children need to have the opportunities to engage in learning in a wide range of settings. An argument for greater opportunities to learn outdoors is not an argument against learning indoors. Goswami's (2008, 2015) neurological research into learning principles describes how incremental learning leads to increasingly complex thought processes and shows that 'certain experiences may result in previously distinct parts of the network becoming connected' (Goswami, 2008, p. 388). In other words the spaces inhabited by young children as they play outside can form connections with learning in other places, too – be that the classroom or the PlayStation – and may provide resonance with the less tangible social development experienced in later life. The spaces inhabited as a child impact on the rest of a person's life and learning.

SPACE IN CONTEXT

Spaces are both real and imagined (Catling and Willy, 2009; Witt, 2013). As children explore physical space they also explore and develop imaginative place. As described before, a bush becomes a den, the space behind a tree becomes the door to a new world. This liberation of imagination provides the foundation for the liberation of communication. Children can play with new words in their new worlds, thus developing language and thinking. Our role as teachers is to provide children with the opportunities to experience outdoor spaces and the opportunities to engage in learning through play, be that free play or structured by the teacher to fulfil some specific learning objectives.

Waite, Evans and Rogers (in Waite, 2011) provide a powerful argument for free play, countering the criticisms of lack of structure, lack of focus and thus learning, and the repetitive nature of much free play, with a child-focused perspective. Children learn to structure their own play and although the focus may not be readily apparent to an adult observer this does not mean that the children are not learning. They describe how adults often interrupt play because it steers away from the adults' learning objectives. Free play allows children to discover their own learning objectives. And repetition is a vital element of learning: of inculcating new knowledge and skills. Free play tends to develop from things that motivate a child and so the teacher can indeed provide some influence by providing motivating ideas and new learning for the children to then explore in their own ways. Csikszentmihalyi (1997) describes a state of 'flow', which occurs when we are totally absorbed in an activity. Many of us will have observed children who are completely lost within their own imaginative world of play – or, for example, being totally absorbed in creating a structure or searching the woodland floor for mini-beasts. Csikszentmihalyi (1997) describes how flow arises when there is the right balance between skill and challenge (see Figure 1.1). This is in strong accord with free-play and Forest School philosophies. Children are left to explore and develop their own challenges and their own level of skill, and subsequently skill acquisition. Csikszentmihalyi describes this as a child's 'expansive tendency made up of instincts for exploring, for enjoying novelty and risk' (1997, p. 1). Any interruption by a teacher may well disrupt the learning flow.

As teachers, one of our roles is to provide opportunities to connect children with the outdoors. A simple walk around the school grounds, or a journey stick adventure (see activity box), can provide the motivation for exploration and the desire to discover, ask questions and find out for themselves. A child who becomes fascinated by a woodlouse crawling over a rotten log who then moves to create their own woodlouse with twigs from the forest floor, or school equipment such as K'nex back in the classroom, and then moves to the library corner to read about woodlice is making a direct connection between play and learning outdoors to play and learning indoors. In this way, outdoor learning is not

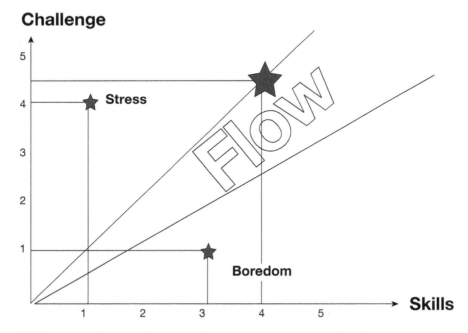

■ **Figure 1.1** The development of flow – or pure concentration – is a balance between skills and challenge (Reproduced with permission from Scoffham, 2013, p. 8)

seen as a 'bolt-on' or something extra, but as an integral part of the child's day of learning in school. The distinction between outdoor and indoor learning is blurred and both are seen as normal learning processes. The following activities can provide the opportunity to make this important blend between learning indoors and outdoors, helping the outdoors to become as much a part of the normal learning space as the classroom.

ACTIVITY BOX **MUSICAL MAPS**

Take your children out to a field, or open area – it can be anywhere that is not totally submerged in the noise of the school or a busy road – and explain to the children that they are going to create a map. However their map is a different type of map. They will create a musical map. Once they enter the musical map area they need to be completely silent, to spread themselves out and find a space on their own and to listen. They put a symbol to represent themselves in the middle of the page and then record all the sounds around them using their own symbols. How far away are the sounds? How loud or soft? Which direction are they from? How long or how short are the sounds? How often repeated? And how can you represent these through symbols on a blank map?

Children's lives are filled with noise – just head outside during playtime and listen – and they really appreciate the opportunity to just stop and listen for a while without distraction. After the initial pause as their ears become accustomed to the sounds, and after the birds are comfortable with their presence, they will be amazed by the sheer range and variety of noises – natural and man-made – that are all around them.

Once the children have had some time to listen and create their maps ask them to find a partner and to share each other's maps. You could add structure here, maybe asking them to use 'Wow' words, or geographical words, for example. This is an important stage. At this point the maps can be used for many learning tasks but as soon as a child is asked to share their map they have to reconfigure their thoughts and communicate them. They have to convert abstract thoughts and patterns and symbols into concrete, verbal communication. They have to describe and justify their ideas, remembering the sounds and the thinking behind their symbols. This leads to an additional layer of learning, particularly for very young children who may need help communicating their thoughts.

■ **Figures 1.2 and 1.3** Reception children listening carefully to the natural sounds around them and creating their own musical map

---

THE CREATIVE SPACE

Outdoor spaces can often be perceived as being a place without boundaries, in a physical sense, but also perhaps in a creative sense too: an imagination unbounded; without walls, without restrictions.

Creativity develops as a process through exploration, be that the exploration of ideas, developing play or using their imagination (Cremin, 2015). Cooper (2013) discusses the key principles of creativity as being: time; possibility and thinking; imagination; risk taking; collaboration; and reaching conclusions. These are considered with reference to teaching outdoors creatively in Box 1.1.

Pascal's research on early years children (2003) identified three core elements of effective learning (Figure 1.4): emotional well-being, a positive disposition to learn and social competence. I believe that regular class learning outside can help children to develop these important learning characteristics.

BOX 1.1 THE KEY PRINCIPLES OF CREATIVITY

Time

Creativity needs time. Children will benefit from space and time to reflect, either individually or by asking questions and discussing in groups.

Time (or the lack of it) is clearly a key component in any school day, but even a short time spent outside can provide the perfect place for reflection and 'taking stock'. In moving out of a busy classroom, stress can be reduced and a child is likely to gain a sense of time and space, even if this is in actual fact quite limited. Indeed a great deal of research (Stigsdotter et al., 2010; Lee and Maheswaran, 2011; Hipp et al., 2015; Cohen-Cline, Turkheimer and Duncan, 2015) points to the positive impact that even a short, regular time spent out in green spaces can have on feelings of well-being.

Possibility and thinking

Payne and Watchow (2009) lead the charge for 'slow pedagogy' (or eco-pedagogy) by arguing for the educational benefits of providing time for children to absorb, discover and investigate their surroundings in order to develop a better sense of self and their place in the world. They argue that too many outdoor activities, and particularly outdoor adventure activities, are harnessed by the same time constraints and targets as much school-based work. They cite John Dewey (1938/1988) and his call for an 'intelligent theory . . . or philosophy of experience', providing children with time to absorb, reflect and think within nature. This eco-pedagogy often occurs naturally within Forest School settings, when children are provided with the freedom to immerse themselves in hunting for sticks, or just sit by the fire and think.

Imagination

There are many definitions and categorisations of play, but it can also be argued that play, being as fluid as the creativity and imagination of the children taking part in it, defies such nomenclatures. I feel that this is even more so in outdoor environments because the rich tapestry of stimuli attracting input from all the senses, coupled with the freedoms and liberation from structure that natural environments both demonstrate and invite, ensures play can flow and evolve in a continual evolution of imagination.

Risk taking

Risk taking does not have to be defined as actual physical risk. The perception of risk is enough for children to feel challenged and subsequently rewarded with success. There is an implication of the novelty of something that is a risk. Once completed a number of times, it is no longer a risk, and it is this new experience that lends itself to the rationale of creativity. Risk does not have to mean risk to body and health, either. The potential of failure is a risk: be that climbing a tree, looking for mini-beasts or designing a new shelter to live in. Children can learn a huge amount through failure: about themselves certainly, but also about coping strategies, about metacognition and about trial and error. This process of reflection can help to make children better learners. Taking risks is a powerful platform for new learning, in a constructivist sense as much as any other, and this is discussed in far greater detail by Lee Pritchard and Colin Wood in chapter 10.

Collaboration

There are certainly opportunities for excellent collaborative work within the classroom and these also exist beyond the classroom walls. Being outdoors brings greater freedom and opportunities to work together, share ideas and discuss learning. There are no walls or ceilings for children's voices to bounce off and around outside. Additionally, many outdoor activities require collaboration and support. Perhaps with fewer non-living support systems: no books or papers, no computers or pencil cases, there is inevitably a great reliance on each other. And this raw state of mutual learning is the foundation for new ideas; for creativity. Stephenson (2002) describes the classroom as being where the teacher manages and directs, but where the outdoors is the child's domain.

(After Cooper, 2013)

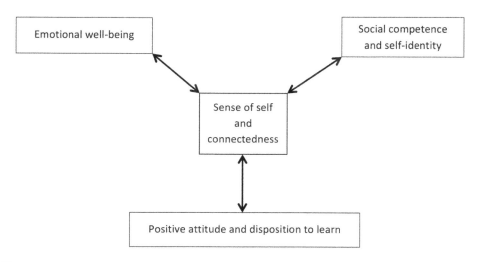

■ **Figure 1.4** What makes an effective learner

(After Pascal, 2003)

There is certainly a wealth of evidential research to support the notion that learning outdoors has a positive effect on children's emotional well-being, even if the mechanisms are not as yet clear, from the 'biophilia' hypotheses (Burns, 1998) and 'ecopsychology' of Roszak, Gomes and Kanner (1995) to the more recent studies such as Hipp et al. (2015) described previously. In 2008 an Ofsted report concluded that: 'When planned and implemented well, learning outside the classroom contributed significantly to raising standards & improving pupils' personal, social & emotional development'.

It is abundantly clear to primary school teachers today that if children arrive at school with a sense of emotional well-being then they are going to be better prepared and motivated to learn and work. On a completely untried and untested piece of research it is worth noting that I have often heard lunchtime supervisors describe how much calmer and less stressful lunchtime monitoring is after the children have returned from a Forest School session!

Children learn social competence through observing others and trying things out for themselves. Picture for a moment a class of children trying a 'high ropes course' during a residential week. Achieving a task that is challenging and requires teamwork clearly helps children to develop social competence, and confidence too. Social competence is not just gained from achieving the challenge, but from the jokes and camaraderie that go with it. These types of activities pay dividends for the teacher. I have always felt that I know my class and all its wonderful individuals so much better after such experiences, and the children respond to you differently too: they see you for the person you are rather than just as their teacher. Social competence for children is as much about responding to adults as it is to their peers.

There are many, many children who are bright and positive and keen to learn throughout their school careers and then through life. There are others, for a broad range of reasons, for whom a positive disposition to learning can be temporal, easily damaged or elusive. There are often external factors outside the control of the teacher or the child that militate against the development of a positive disposition. It is clear that having a positive attitude to learning will help children to learn better but it is sometimes less easy to see how such positive attitudes can be supported and developed; and how we can help children develop resilience. The chapters throughout this book are full of activities, ideas and thinking that motivate children and enliven learning. I fully support the view that regular learning outside the classroom through a range of activities will, over time, help children to develop as motivated, interested children who wish to learn and discover, and who develop a growing resilience to issues and difficulties that they may meet through their lives.

If children feel a connection with the environment they inhabit they will undoubtedly feel more secure. And with security comes a feeling of assuredness. Children naturally have a strong connection with their home environment and teachers work hard to make their school a safe and secure environment too. As children get older their sphere of influence expands to friends' houses, family members and their homes and to the local places they explore. This natural expansion of space is to be encouraged because a sense of connectedness with their local area and home environment will aid well-being, a sense of security and a sense of place in the world.

REACHING CONCLUSIONS

What is the difference between creativity and imagination? Well, one answer is that whilst imagination may not need to lead anywhere, creativity has to be linked to creating something, to reaching a conclusion (NACCCE, 1999). For outdoor learning to be purposeful learning, the children involved need to be motivated by the work they are engaged with and also need to understand the reason why they are undertaking such work. A lack of conclusion, or resolution, can ultimately prove to be disengaging as children will start to question the reason for such activities. What I assume teachers want from creative learning outdoors is for children to be able to develop learning skills and so it is always worthwhile in plenaries to focus on *how* answers and outcomes were reached rather than just *what* answers and outcomes were reached. If children can be given the opportunities to transfer the learning and knowledge gained between work completed indoors and that completed outdoors then they will develop as more effective learners.

If children are afforded space to explore then the creative possibilities become richer. If you take a look at an early years classroom you will see the environment is full of opportunities for creative play and learning. Children have open access to many resources and a short visit will often result in observing some children involved in construction, others in role play and some in art and craft. Everything is at hand, everything in place and many things are possible. Now I want you to transpose that setting into the outside. The resources that fire children's interests can be found easily through a range of natural materials. There will be the same potential for discovery and role play and much of an

---

ACTIVITY BOX **JOURNEY STICKS**

Children can be taken on a journey to help them appreciate, discover and map out the outdoor area beyond their classrooms. 'Journey sticks' (Catling, 2004; Palfrey, 2004; Whittle, 2006) is a wonderful device that enables children to explore their local area in a focused manner and then discuss and make use of the exploration back in the classroom.

In its simplest form each child, or pair, walks through a woodland or natural area with a stick that they have found (not a large stick, perhaps half a metre). As a teacher you will need to walk with them armed with cotton, string, sellotape, scissors and any other resources you feel you may need to help the children attach things they find to their stick – like paper for bark rubbings. As the children walk around they collect things to add to their stick. Encourage them to talk about the things they find and where they find them as they walk. This will help them to remember so when they get back to the classroom, for example, they will be able to tell you that they found the fluffy white feather just by the huge gnarly tree as they turned left.

Back at the classroom the children's sticks – covered in memories from their walk – can be used as discussion points about things you can find and children can use the stick to develop a map of the area they have walked on, or to create a story based on the things they have found. They can be encouraged to attach feelings to the things that they found – intrigue, happiness, wonder. . . – and these feelings can be added to their map using symbols.

Journey sticks help children to develop a sense of place through understanding maps and routes. Here the children create a map with a purpose, as it is a map to mark their journey, with signs and symbols developed from the objects that they have collected. Children will develop communication skills and story making skills by describing their route, using the journey stick as a guide, and by making up stories based around the objects they have found.

early years classroom can be replicated in the outside world. But there is a significant difference with natural environments when you consider provision for learning through play. A classroom is full of toys that mimic real life – dolls and figures, houses and toy cars – whilst natural areas like woodlands contain none of these. There is a strong argument that using inanimate objects, like sticks, leaves or stones, fosters greater imagination. A doll can be a doll, but some twigs can be a doll or an aeroplane or a magic wand or whatever a child wants it to be . . . (Steiner, 1965).

ACTIVITY BOX **WE'RE GOING ON A BEAR HUNT!**

We're Going on a Bear Hunt (Rosen, 1989) needs no introduction – it is a book everyone knows and loves. Children love the repetitive poetry of the words and the expectation of the bear. It resonates with family and adventure. It is a fun book of familial safety with a light-hearted scare. Children like to be safely scared. And significantly for us, it takes children on a walk across a range of terrain which may not all be easily accessible, but some of the pages will show a familiar, local landscape to many children. So take the children out on their own bear hunt! As the children walk through the paths of their own bear hunt encourage them to collect natural materials that represent the various environments they walk through: a few twigs to represent the stumble trip roots of the trees, a handful of grass for the swishy swashy grass . . . can the children be inventive with their own bear hunt? And the walk – once they have found the bear of course – will enable children to make their own map of their route using all the natural materials that they have picked up along the way.

This is a super activity to forge a bridge between the classroom, reading the story and using literature, art and the outside spaces, to make sense of the story: re-creating the story by building from children's imaginations, and in the process developing a sense of place and a desire to explore. And the work can then be brought into the classroom to be developed further.

REFERENCES

Bandura, A. (1977) *Social Learning Theory*. New Jersey, Prentice Hall.

Bandura, A. (1997) *Self-efficacy: The Exercise of Control*. New York, Freeman Publishing.

Burns, G.W. (1998) *Nature-Guided Therapy – Brief Integrative Strategies for Health and Well-Being*. Philadelphia, Brunner/Mazel.

Catling, S. (2004) *Primary Geography Handbook Extension Project – Maps and Stories (4–7)*. Available at: www.geography.org.uk/projects/primaryhandbook/mapsandstories/4-7 (accessed 17 November 2016).

Catling, S. and Willy, T. (2009) *Teaching Primary Geography*. Exeter, Learning Matters.

Cohen-Cline, H., Turkheimer, E. and Duncan, G.E. (2015) Access to green space, physical activity and mental health: a twin study. *Journal of Epidemiology and Community Health* 69: 523–529.

Cooper, H. (2013) *Teaching History Creatively*. London, Routledge.

Cremin, T. (2015) *Teaching English Creatively*. Oxon, Routledge.

Csikszentmihalyi, M. (1997) *Creativity: Flow and the Psychology of Discovery and Invention*. London, Harper Perennial.

Dewey, J. (1938/1988) Experience and education. In Payne, P. and Wattchow, B. (2009) Phenomenological deconstruction, slow pedagogy, and the corporeal turn in wild environmental/outdoor education. *Canadian Journal of Environmental Education*, 14.

Goswami, U. (2008) Principles of learning, implications for teaching: a cognitive neuroscience perspective. *Journal of Philosophy of Education*, 42, 3–4.

Goswami, U. (2015) *Children's Cognitive Development And Learning CPRT Research Survey 3* (new series) Cambridge Primary Review Trust. Cambridge, Pearson.

Gray, C. and MacBlain, S. (2015) *Learning Theories in Childhood*. London, Sage.

Hipp, J.A., Gulwadi, G.B., Alves, S. and Sequira, S. (2015) The relationship between perceived greenness and perceived restorativeness of university campuses and student-reported quality of life. *Environment and Behavior*: 1–17.

House of Commons Children, Schools and Families Committee (2010) *Transforming Education Outside the Classroom*. London, the Stationary Office Limited.

Lee, A.C.K. and Maheswaran, R. (2011) The health benefits of urban green spaces: a review of the evidence. *Journal of Public Health* 33, 2: 212–222.

NACCCE (1999) *All Our Futures: Creativity, Culture and Education. Report to the Secretary of State for Education and Employment, the Secretary of State for Culture, Media and Sport*. London, NACCCE.

Ofsted (2008) *Learning Outside the Classroom. How Far Should You Go?* London, HMSO.

Palfrey, D. (2004) TTA funded workshop organised by PENAC (Primary Educators Network for the Advancement of Citizenship). Available at: www.citized.info/pdf/conferences/Citizenship_Humanities_Agenda.pdf (accessed 17 November 2016).

Pascal, C. (2003) Effective early learning: an act of practical theory. *European Early Childhood Education Research Journal* 11, 2: 7–28.

Payne, P. and Wattchow, B. (2009) Phenomenological deconstruction, slow pedagogy, and the corporeal turn in wild environmental/outdoor education. *Canadian Journal of Environmental Education*, 14.

Rosen, M. (1989) *We're Going on a Bear Hunt*. London, McEldery Books.

Roszak, T., Gomes, M.E. and Kanner, A.D. (eds) (1995) *Ecopsychology: Restoring the Earth, Healing the Mind*. San Francisco, CA, Sierra Club Books.

Rouse, E. (2015) Mixed-age grouping in early childhood – creating the outdoor learning environment. *Early Child Development and Care* 185, 5: 742–751.

Scoffham, S. (ed.) (2013) *Teaching Geography Creatively*. Oxon, Routledge.

Steiner, R. (1965, re-published 1995) *The Education of the Child in the Light of Anthroposophy*. Rudolf Steiner Publishing. Available at: http://wn.rsarchive.org/Articles/GA034/English/RSP1965/EduChi_index.html (accessed 17 November 2016).

Stephenson, A. (2002) Opening up the outdoors: exploring the relationship between the indoor and the outdoor environment of a centre. *Early Childhood Education Research* 10: 29–38.

Stigsdotter, U.K., Ekholm, O., Schipperijn, J., Toftager, M., Kamper-Jorgenson, F. and Randrup, T.B. (2010) Health promoting outdoor environments – associations between green space, and health, health-related quality of life and stress based on a Danish national representative survey. *Scandinavian Journal of Public Health* 38,4: 411–417.

Waite, C. (2011) *Children Learning Outside the Classroom*. London, Sage.

Whittle, J. (2006) Journey sticks and affective mapping. *Primary Geographer* 59. Sheffield, Geographical Association.

Witt, S. (2013) Chapter 4. In Scoffham, S. (ed.) *Teaching Geography Creatively*. Oxon, Routledge, pp. 44–58.

TAKING THE LEARNING OUTDOORS AT KS1

Extending early years practice for 5 to 7 year olds

Julia Tanner

This chapter investigates the potential and possibilities for extending good Early Years practice in working outdoors for children aged five to seven years (KS1 in England). The first section focuses on the principles of good practice in the education of young children, including the specific benefits of outdoor learning. The second section of the chapter focuses on strategies for enhancing learning in KS1 by taking the learning outdoors. It is presented in two parts. First, I offer suggestions for auditing your current practice in outdoor learning, including identifying the possibilities of your specific situation and observing and consulting children. Second, I suggest some starting points for taking learning outside, addressing practical issues, considering how outdoor work can enrich learning across the curriculum and suggesting some easy starting points for enhancing the outdoor environment.

Creativity can be seen as 'a property of people (who we are), a process (what we do), or products (what we make)' (Fisher, 2004, p. 8). It is defined by the National Advisory Committee on Creative and Cultural Education (NACCCE) as 'imaginative activity fashioned so as to yield an outcome that is of value as well as original' (NACCCE, 1999, p. 29). Throughout this chapter, I encourage you to reflect on how you can think creatively about the enormous potential of outdoor learning, and on how you can ensure that the children you teach are able enjoy the unique learning opportunities afforded by taking learning outdoors.

EARLY YEARS PRINCIPLES AND PRACTICE

The early years are recognised as a time of extraordinary development which can lay the foundations for later learning and for a happy, productive and fulfilling life. They are a critical period characterised by rapid physical, cognitive, social and emotional development.

From birth, remarkable transformations occur in young children's physical, cognitive and socio-emotional abilities. These transformations mark the progressive acquisition of skills and capacities, in terms of developing relationships, communicating with others, play and learning. Consequently, early childhood is seen as a uniquely sensitive period of life requiring particular care, attention and support (UNESCO, 2006). Historically, early years pioneers such as Pestalozzi, Froebel and Margaret McMillan recognised the unique nature of early childhood and argued for an informal play-led approach including outdoor play (Joyce, 2012).

Subsequent research in developmental psychology has revealed that young children's physical, cognitive, social and emotional functioning differs from that of older children. Based on this research, and on current understanding of the psychological and sociocultural factors which influence developmental processes, the National Association for the Education of Young Children (NAEYC) has proposed twelve principles of 'developmentally appropriate practice' for children from birth to eight years (NAEYC, 2009). These are detailed in Box 2.1.

Internationally, most early years care and education for young children is based on the premise that they are curious about themselves, other people, things and the world, and that their learning is best fostered by a child-led approach. Bertram and Pascal (2002) reviewed the early years' curriculum, pedagogical and assessment approaches of twenty countries across the world and found that they share many features in common. Stephen, for example, notes that early years curricula typically 'share an holistic view of learning and the learner, stress active or experiential learning, respect children's ability to be self-motivating and directing and value responsive interactions between children and adults as crucial for learning' (Stephen, 2006, p. 15). These curricula reflect a belief in developmentally appropriate practice, based on contemporary understandings of child development

BOX 2.1 TWELVE PRINCIPLES OF DEVELOPMENTALLY APPROPRIATE PRACTICE FOR CHILDREN AGED 0–8 YEARS

- All domains of development and learning – physical, social and emotional, and cognitive – are related.
- Children follow well-documented sequences to build knowledge.
- Children develop and learn at varying rates.
- Learning develops from the dynamic interaction of biological maturation and experience.
- Early childhood experiences can have profound effects, and optimal periods exist for certain types of development and learning.
- Development proceeds toward greater complexity and self-regulation.
- Children thrive with secure, consistent relationships with responsive adults.
- Multiple social and cultural contexts influence learning and development.
- Children learn in a variety of ways, so teachers need a range of strategies.
- Play helps develop self-regulation, language, cognition and social competence.
- Children advance when challenged just beyond their current level of mastery.
- Children's experiences shape their motivation, which in turn affects their learning.

(NAEYC, 2009)

and learning, the uniqueness of each individual child, and the importance of the social and cultural contexts in which children live, grow and develop (NAEYC, 2009).

Outdoor learning is seen as an integral element of developmentally appropriate practice in early childhood. Froebel coined the term 'kindergarten' (literally, a garden for children) in the early nineteenth century, and the name is still used in many parts of the world for early education settings. For Froebel, the 'garden for children' was both an actual place for children to play and learn together, and a metaphor for a rich environment where adults could nurture children's healthy growth and development, as gardeners tend plants (Tovey, 2007, p. 40). Progressive pioneers who followed Froebel, such as Montessori, McMillan, Steiner and Isaacs, all believed that regular access to outdoors was essential for children's development and learning. They championed the importance of the outdoor environment by recognising its potential for fostering children's independence, encouraging active learning, offering first hand experiences, ensuring contact with nature and providing opportunities for risk taking and adventurousness (Tovey, 2007, pp. 50–51).

Following this tradition, in the UK, outdoor learning is well established in pre-school settings. The Statutory Framework for the Early Years Foundation Stage (EYFS) in England states that 'Providers must provide access to an outdoor play area or, if that is not possible, ensure that outdoor activities are planned and taken on a daily basis' (DfE, 2014). Consequently, good practice in the EYFS means that children have regular access to an outdoor space, that indoor and outdoor learning take place simultaneously, that outdoor and indoor learning complement each other and are seen as equally important and challenging, and that children are encouraged to be active, creative, exploratory and independent in both environments (Bryce-Clegg, 2013; Moylett, 2013; Wood, 2013; Nutbrown and Clough, 2014). However, there is a marked reduction as children move from EYFS to KS1 (Sharp, 2006; Waite, 2010).

The 'powerful arguments for taking every opportunity to take young children beyond their immediate indoor environment' are summarised by the Council for Learning Outside the Classroom. They argue that:

■ Learning outside the classroom supports the development of healthy and active lifestyles by offering children opportunities for physical activity, freedom and movement, and promoting a sense of well-being.

■ Learning outside the classroom gives children contact with the natural world and offers them experiences that are unique to the outdoors, such as direct contact with the weather and the seasons.

■ Playing and learning outside also help children to understand and respect nature, the environment and the interdependence of humans, animals, plants and lifecycles.

■ Outdoor play also supports children's problem-solving skills and nurtures their creativity, as well as providing rich opportunities for their developing imagination, inventiveness and resourcefulness.

■ Children need an outdoor environment that can provide them with space, both upwards and outwards, and places to explore, experiment, discover, be active and healthy, and to develop their physical capabilities.

■ The outdoor environment offers space and therefore is particularly important to those children who learn best through active movement. Very young children learn predominantly through their sensory and physical experiences, which support brain development and the creation of neural networks.

■ For many children, playing outdoors at their early years setting may be the only opportunity they have to play safely and freely while they learn to assess risk and develop the skills to manage new situations.

■ Learning that flows seamlessly between indoors and outdoors makes the most efficient use of resources and builds on interests and enthusiasms.

■ Anyone who takes children outside regularly sees the enjoyment and sense of wonder and excitement that is generated when children actively engage with their environment.

(Council for Learning Outside the Classroom, 2009)

These arguments rest on the premise that the outdoor learning environment is qualitatively different from the indoor classroom. Gibson suggested that different environments have different affordances – what they offer or provide in terms of potential for action (Gibson, 1977). For example, a beach may offer the children the opportunity to paddle in the sea, feel the sand squelch up between their toes, build sandcastles, investigate rock pools, observe the patterns the waves leave in the sand and collect shells; while an urban park will offer different possibilities, such as playing on the swings, feeding ducks on the pond, spotting butterflies and bees on the flowers and exploring behind the cricket club pavilion.

The differences between the affordances of indoor and outdoor learning environments are stark. Outdoors, children have fresh air, more space, contact with the changing natural world and often access to very different equipment and resources, which together create a rich context for learning. As White argues, outdoor learning offers children the space 'to be their natural, exuberant physical and noisy selves' (2014, p. 3), where they can fully engage their bodies as well as their brains (Ouvrey, 2003). The outdoors environment provides many opportunities for learning that simply cannot be replicated inside (Bilton, 2010; Tovey, 2007; White, 2014).

Why is it important to continue outdoor learning in KS1?

Chapter 1, amongst others, reviews the proven benefits of outdoor learning including positive impacts on children and young people's educational attainment, motivation, social and emotional wellbeing and physical health (Rickinson et al., 2004; Ofsted, 2008; Dillon and Dickie, 2012; Rickinson et al., 2012). Here, I provide a rationale for continuing outdoor learning from EYFS into KS1.

Developmentally, there is very little difference between under-fives and KS1 children. Instead, child development literature tends to emphasise the continuing need for concrete, first hand, practical learning experiences, at least partly rooted in play, for this age group (Fisher, 2010; Whitebread, 2012). Reviewing the literature and drawing on her own observations and KS1 teachers' experience, Fisher (2010) suggests that Y1 and Y2 children learn best when

■ learning is natural and spontaneous, including being inquisitive, messy and creative and open-ended;

■ children are given time and space to be active and to see an activity through to completion;

■ children are motivated by a rich environment offering new experiences, choice and variety, independence and fun;

- leaning is supported by knowledgeable adults who intervene appropriately and respond positively to children's contributions;
- alongside peers, talking, negotiating and testing out ideas together;
- initiating their own enquiries, drawing on their own experiences and pursuing their own interests;
- children are able to rehearse, repeat and revisit learning activities and experiences;
- the learning environment is relaxed and supportive, children feel happy and cared for and relationships are good;
- children are engaged and involved because learning is relevant, meaningful, and challenging, and they are encouraged to use their own initiative.

(Fisher, 2010, pp. 28–32)

These general principles about how 5–7 year olds best learn clearly demonstrate that outdoor learning remains developmentally appropriate, important and necessary for children as they move from the EYFS and into KS1. Outdoor learning is powerful because it is experiential (Kolb, 1984). It motivates children and young people by offering direct, first hand learning experiences in a real life context. It integrates kinaesthetic, cognitive and affective learning, making it memorable. As Moffett argues,

All forms of outdoor learning provide direct experience with the natural world; outdoor learning is real learning and can therefore help to bring school subjects to life; outdoor learning is active and involves participants in *learning through what they do, encounter and discover*.

(Moffett, 2011, p. 278, my italics)

As all KS1 teachers know, 5–7 year olds still need plenty of opportunities to learn by 'doing, encountering and discovering'. Imagine the difference for a 6 year old between learning about biodiversity by listening to a teacher while watching a whiteboard presentation, or going out into the school grounds armed with a pooter, magnifying glass and recording sheet to investigate the mini-beasts living under logs, in the soil and on the flowering shrubs.

The affordances of the outdoor learning environment and the greater freedom children have in it also seem important for unleashing children's natural creativity. Outdoors, children play and learn with greater energy, intensity, imagination and cooperation (Waite et al., 2011). Research consistently suggests that the outdoor environment offers more opportunities for self-directed learning, and that because children are often freer of adult supervision, there are greater opportunities for them to make choices about activities, locations and social groupings (Davis et al., 2006). This, together with the space to work messily, noisily and at a large scale, appears to foster creative and imaginative thought. Outside, children will often make creative use of specific available environmental features (such as trees, corners, steps or doorways) using ingenuity and resourcefulness to transform them into contexts for imaginative play.

The first part of this chapter focuses on the benefits of taking the learning outdoors for children aged 5–7 years. It argues that, developmentally, children of this age need regular access to outdoor learning as much as those under 5 years. It meets their needs for active experiential learning and supports all aspects of their physical, cognitive, social and emotional development. It provides a rich context for cross-curricular learning and the

---

ACTIVITY BOX **DEVELOPING OUTDOOR LEARNING**

Outdoor learning audit

As a starting point for auditing your current situation, you might like to consider these questions:

- What do you see as the benefits of taking more learning outside for the children?
- What sorts of learning do you already take outside?
- What do the children think about outdoor learning?
- What access do you have to the outdoors?
- What is the outdoor learning environment like?
- How can your school grounds creatively support learning across the curriculum?
- What do you see as the benefits of taking more learning outside for the children?

---

space for exuberant movement, noisy and messy activities, and large-scale projects. The outdoor environment provides a unique context for learning about the natural world. Young children are naturally drawn to the outdoors, and enjoy it. Finally, research shows that outdoor learning has positive impacts on children's physical and emotional health, on their educational achievement and on their social and interpersonal skills.

If you wish to develop more outdoor learning, it is important that you articulate a personal rationale for it. You may need to consider how to persuade different stakeholders – your colleagues, your senior leadership team and parents and carers – of its benefits. Which of these arguments seem most pertinent in your school? Which of them will be most persuasive with these diverse stakeholders groups?

Which types of learning do you already take outside?

It is very likely that you already do take some learning outside. Almost all KS1 children do some PE outside, and have the chance to occasionally enjoy stories outside on a warm summer afternoon. You may have used the school grounds for specific activities such as exploring different habitats in Science, using seasonal change as inspiration for poetry writing (English) or investigating how an aerial photograph shows the site of the school in Geography.

These typical activities represent a starting point for developing outdoor learning. They are good examples of how you can exploit the unique qualities of the outdoor learning environment. Considering what sort of learning you already take outside, and when, will also provide an opportunity to reflect on children's response to learning outside.

What do children think about outdoor learning?

We often think of playtime as a time for children to 'run off' excess energy built up during more sedentary time spend in the classroom, and indeed, many of them do engage in physically active play such as chasing games. However, if you observe the playground carefully, you will probably find many children chatting with friends, engaged in imaginative role play, exploring the environment or playing singing/clapping games.

Observing children in self-chosen unstructured activities can be very instructive about their natural response to being outdoors, as these 'play' activities offer abundant learning opportunities.

Research suggests that most children and young people respond positively to outdoor learning (White, 2014, p. 2). The reduction in outdoor learning is one of the changes children moving from EYFS to KS1 most often comment on. A small-scale action research project undertaken in an urban primary school revealed that slightly older children (aged 8–9 years) were overwhelmingly positive about outdoor learning. They remembered the lessons they had been taught outside, and were eager for more. They had relished opportunities to 'take the learning outside', appreciated the rich potential of learning in the school grounds for work across the curriculum and especially valued the space and fresh air outdoor learning afforded (Whawell and Tanner, 2015).

There are a number of ways you could investigate your class's perspectives on outdoor learning, including:

- invite small groups to brainstorm their memories of outdoor learning;
- organise a whole class discussion about what the children see as the advantages and disadvantages of outdoor learning;
- ask a group to conduct a class survey of favourite outdoor activities;
- make a class book involving contributions from all children, about 'learning outdoors';
- provide a camera for children to take images of places they think could help their learning in the school grounds, and discuss why they chose these particular places.

Clark and Moss (2001, 2005) provide detailed advice for consulting young children, and strategies for engaging them in subsequent decision making about outdoor learning are offered through Learning Through Landscapes (n.d.).

What access do you have to the outdoors?

Access to the outdoors is partly a matter of physical access, and partly a matter of school culture, i.e. the extent to which taking the learning outdoors is part of ordinary practice in your school. If you are lucky, you will have a classroom with an outside door that leads directly into the school grounds. If not, you may have to go through a cloakroom or shared area, or along a corridor. Obviously, straightforward easy direct access is desirable, but many schools have found imaginative solutions to access problems, such as KS1 classes sharing EYFS outdoor space, moving KS1 classes to the rooms with the best access or creating new external doorways (Fisher, 2010, p. 125).

What is the outdoor learning environment like?

School grounds vary hugely, but all offer potential for developing outdoor learning. You could start by walking round your school site. Consider its features and its potential as a dynamic and rich learning environment. You might like to take a camera and a large-scale map, so that you can record what you find. If you undertake this activity with colleagues, you will find that together, you notice more than you would by yourself. This is also an excellent way of building shared commitment to outdoor learning.

When surveying your grounds, notice which of these features you have, and their location:

- hard landscaping – different surfaces and materials;
- different levels, gradients and slopes;
- boundaries – hedges, walls, fences;
- shelter – from the sun, rain and wind;
- plants – trees, bushes, flowers, grass;
- soil, rocks and stones, and any other natural materials;
- access to water (outside taps) and drainage;
- storage facilities;
- permanent structures (sheds, outbuildings, greenhouses);
- different zones – playground, grass, carpark, nature area, pond, kitchen service areas, etc.

Together, the features of your school grounds will offer a unique environment, full of potential for supporting and enhancing children's learning.

How can your school grounds creatively support learning across the curriculum?

As you audit your school grounds and the available learning resources, make a note of how they offer opportunities directly related to the curriculum you offer, whether this is organised in discreet subjects or through more integrated themes, topics or enquiries. If you work with a specified curriculum, such as the National Curriculum for England (DfE, 2013), you might like to systematically review each curriculum area. Alternatively, you could work with colleagues to annotate your medium term plans with possible ideas, or simply note possibilities that occur to you for incorporating outdoor learning in your plans for the next week or fortnight.

Once you have completed your initial audit, you should have identified the specific affordances of your school grounds as a site for learning and plenty of opportunities for taking the learning outdoors across the curriculum and also be in a much stronger position to identify your immediate and longer term development priorities.

TAKING THE LEARNING OUTDOORS IN KS1

Many KS1 teachers appreciate the value of outdoor learning, but find that practical issues constrain them from exploiting its full potential. Issues often raised as stumbling blocks include staffing, storage and the curriculum. In this section I explore some possible creative solutions for addressing these issues.

Staffing

You may need to think creatively about staffing and supervision issues! However you approach this issue, you need to consult your Senior Leadership Team and work within relevant school policies. Guidance on risk management is provided by Lindon (2011) and Beames et al. (2012, pp. 77–92). Many whole class activities (e.g. PE, story, clay work, music composition) make no more staffing demands outdoors than indoors. Some classrooms have direct access to an adjacent safe outdoors space where children can be seen from inside or one can be created by fencing off a designated area. In these cases, especially if you want to encourage the independence and autonomy fostered by outdoor learning, you may not need to have an adult outside. You can build children's sense of responsibility for keeping themselves safe through discussion and by creating a class set of 'Outdoor Learning Rules'. Alternatively, if you share an outdoor space with colleagues, consider how the whole staff team can best be deployed to provide as much support for outdoor learning as possible. Outdoor learning in small groups can be facilitated by teachers and support staff alike.

Storage of outdoor learning resources

Most schools have a wide range of resources which could be used to support creative outdoor learning if they were made available for use outdoors. These include much standard KS1 classroom equipment such as writing materials, art and craft materials and tools, books, large and small construction, small world figures, measuring equipment, natural materials (stones, shells and feathers), role play clothes and props, clipboards and IT equipment. In addition, some more specialised resources such as PE equipment (hoops, bean bags and balls) or musical instruments are often used more creatively if they are taken outdoors.

Appropriate storage arrangements for resources are essential. As in the classroom, resources to support outdoor learning need to be well organised, attractively presented, accessible to children and carefully maintained. Initially, plastic boxes with lids are an excellent storage solution. These can be labelled and used to store portable resources and tools. They can be kept indoors in the classroom or cloakroom, and simply taken outside when needed. Children can learn to take responsibility for using equipment with care, and returning it to its proper place when they have finished with it. In the long run, you may wish to work towards acquiring a shed or outbuilding with low level, labelled shelving which facilitates children's independent use of outdoor learning resources.

Learning across the curriculum

Start by considering the opportunities you have for simply taking what could otherwise be classroom learning outside. Could you choose to take circle time, singing, phonics, story or times table practice outside? Could 'Golden Time' include the chance to take a book, puppet or small world play figures outside? Is it possible for some learning to 'spill out' of the classroom, allowing children the benefit of fresh air and more space?

Remember, too, that wherever you are, your school grounds are full of potential for direct learning from the outdoor environment, whether it is identifying different materials (Science), finding and naming shapes (Maths), using a map (Geography), observing evidence of change (History) or drawing a flower from observation (Art). You should also consider when the additional space available outdoors would enhance children's learning by allowing them to engage in messier, noisier or larger scale activities than would be possible indoors. For example, outside, children can use messy materials such as papier-mâché and clay, construct large 3D sculptures, experiment with loud musical instruments or singing games, make dens big enough for several children and create extensive fantasy model worlds.

Outdoor learning facilitates independent active learning, problem-solving, collaborative working and creative thinking (White, 2014:3), so think about how you can capitalise on these in setting open ended learning tasks which challenge the children to take responsibility for planning and completing activities themselves. Box 2.2, modelled on the National Trust's initiative of '50 Things to do Outdoors before you're 11¾' (National Trust, n.d.) suggests 50 challenges for KS1 children to undertake in their school grounds.

Finally, consider what you can do to enhance your school grounds to create an even richer, more dynamic outdoor learning environment. Many changes can be made fairly quickly and without much expense. For example, you could

- enhance planting and/or add moveable planters;
- make some raised beds for gardening;
- change mowing regimes to create long grass areas;
- create wildlife habitats with bird boxes or bug hotels, hedges and log heaps;
- plant some trees;
- provide natural materials (tree trunks, circles of wood, sticks, stones, etc.);
- install some tables and seating;
- mount blackboards and whiteboards on playground walls;
- work with the children to devise, create and install art works.

CONCLUSION

The resurgence of interest in outdoor learning for all age groups in education in recent years has been fuelled by concerns about the nature of contemporary childhood (e.g. Palmer, 2007). In the Western world, children and young people are leading increasingly sedentary indoor based lives, with less access to green spaces and less free, unsupervised outdoor play opportunities compared to previous generations. Concerns about the impact of sedentary lifestyles focus on the impact on children's physical and emotional well-being, and on their sense of stewardship for the environment (Charles and Louv, 2009).

As I have argued, the arguments for continuing to offer KS1 children outdoor learning are compelling. Developmentally, 5 and 6 year olds want and need similar experiences to EYFS children, and we know that outdoor learning continues to be important to them. Contemporary experts in early childhood, such as Tovey (2007), Fisher (2010), Broadhead et al. (2010) and White (2014), all argue that such provision offers young children unique and essential learning opportunities which simply cannot be replicated indoors in the classroom. Their championing of outdoor learning into KS1 is rooted in the notion of developmentally appropriate practice and an understanding of the unique affordances of the outdoors as a learning environment for this age group. As Bayley, Broadbent and Featherstone (2011) insist,

> Children in Key Stage 1 need and deserve the chance to build on the best of practice in the EYFS, which carefully balances adult directed tasks with learning that children initiate and develop themselves, often in the company of responsive adults. These activities, which include sand and water play, construction, role play, independent mark making and writing, creative work, dance and movement, and *outdoor play*, are some of the activities children value most and miss most in Years 1 and 2.
>
> (Bayley et al., 2011, p. 4, my italics)

BOX 2.2 50 THINGS TO DO IN THE SCHOOL GROUNDS BEFORE YOU ARE 7 AND ¾

- Build a home for pixies to live in.
- Imagine how the school grounds will look in fifty years.
- Plant some seeds or bulbs in a pattern and watch the pattern emerge as they grow.
- Create some environmental art using natural materials such as grass, sticks and leaves.
- Chalk a road layout for model vehicles on the playground.
- Go on a mini-beast safari, then design and make your own model mini-beast and find a home for it in the school grounds.
- Design a maths trail focusing on shape, numbers or symmetry for your class to do.
- Make up a game using a directional compass.
- Find the highest place you can safely stand.
- Invent a singing and clapping game and teach it to your friends.
- Make up a photo-story using a doll, puppet or model animal as the main character, and the grounds as the story setting.
- Design and build a den.
- Find some things that smell, and experiment with making perfume with them.
- Use an audio recorder to record sounds you find in the school grounds, and edit these together to create a soundscape.
- Discover something that is hidden.
- Mix soil and water to make a liquid and use large brushes to paint a picture on the playground.
- Design and set up a role-play area for an outdoor place such as a beach, a bird hide at a nature reserve, or a café at a garden centre.
- Turn part of your school grounds into a poetry garden.
- Create a new playground game with a ball and some hoops.
- Collect some natural objects and use them to make a seasonal collage.
- Choose a colour and see how many shades of that colour you can find. Then paint a picture using only the shades you found.
- Find the best place to sit and read a book with your friend.
- Create a treasure hunt for your class.
- Decorate a stick to turn it into a magic wand, then use it to cast spells.
- Invent a new version of a traditional children's game such as Hopscotch, Tag and French Skipping
- Build a tiny snowman.
- Use the outdoor environment as the setting for a puppet play.
- Do some weaving with plant material such as grass or willow.
- Imagine you are a bird flying over the school and describe what you can see.
- Design and make a wind vane and use it to investigate wind direction and speed.
- Play with making shadows on a sunny day.
- Experiment with using your body to move in different ways.
- Use leaves or flowers to make a head garland or bracelet.
- Use chalk to draw around your friend's body, and then turn them into a superhero by drawing them an awesome costume.

■ Choose a small flower, study it carefully through a magnifying glass, then use crayons or pastels to make a huge picture of it.
■ Find the oldest thing in the school grounds.
■ Pretend to be an insect or a small animal exploring the school grounds.
■ Take some photographs and create a montage of images of the school grounds.
■ Use musical instruments to compose a piece of music.
■ Collect some stones or other natural materials and find out how many ways you can sort them into different groups.
■ With your friends, make up a new ending to a traditional story, and then act it out to friends.
■ Lie on the grass and look for pictures in the clouds.
■ Design an experiment to find out what happens to rain when it falls on different surfaces.
■ Make a map of the school grounds on an A2 piece of paper, and use colours or labels to show how you feel about different places.
■ With some friends, choose an important historical event, make some props and act out what happened.
■ Make a large sculpture using junk material and place it in the school grounds.
■ Use natural materials such as grass, sticks, tree roots and stones to create an environment for model animals.
■ Decorate a tree.
■ Make up and tell a story about the day an alien landed in the school grounds.
■ Predict what will happen to an apple core, banana skin or orange peel if it is left outside and observe how it decays over a day, a week, a month.

Children aged 5–7 years want and need first hand learning experiences which ignite their curiosity, provoke questions, challenge their problem-solving skills and satisfy their desire for active investigation and movement. Complementing indoor learning with outdoor learning meets these needs, harnessing children's natural vitality, energy and enthusiasm for being outside. Above all, it promotes their enjoyment of and engagement with learning.

REFERENCES

Bayley, R., Broadbent, L. and Featherstone, S. (2011) *Carrying on in Key Stage 1: Outdoor Play*. London, A&C Black Publishers.

Beames, S., Higgins, P. and Nicol, R. (2012) *Learning Outside the Classroom: Theory and Guidelines for Practice*. London, Routledge.

Bilton, H. (2010) *Outdoor Learning in the Early Years*. London, Routledge.

Bertram, T. and Pascal, C. (2002) *Early Years Education: An International Perspective*. London, Qualifications and Curriculum Authority.

Broadhead, P., Howard, J. and Wood, E. (2010) *Play and Learning in the Early Years: From Research To Practice*. London, Sage.

Bryce-Clegg, A. (2013) *Continuous Provision in the Early Years (Practitioners' Guides)*. London, Bloomsbury.

Charles, C. and Louv, R. (2009) *Children's Nature Deficit: What We Know – and Don't Know*. Available at: www.childrenandnature.org/wp-content/uploads/2015/04/CNNEvidenceof theDeficit.pdf (retrieved 20 June 2016).

Clark, A. and Moss, P. (2001) *Listening to Young Children: The Mosaic Approach.* London, National Children's Bureau.

Clark, A. and Moss, P. (2005) *Spaces to Play: More Listening to Young Children Using the Mosaic Approach.* London, National Children's Bureau.

Council for Learning Outside the Classroom (2009) *Benefits for Early Years of Learning Outside the Classroom.* Available at: www.lotc.org.uk/wp-content/uploads/2010/12/Benefits-for-Early-Years-LOtC-Final-5AUG09.pdf (retrieved 19 June 2016).

Davis, B., Rea, T. and Waite, S. (2006) The special nature of the outdoors: its contribution to the education of children aged 3–11. *Australian Journal of Outdoor Education,* 10(2), 3–12.

Department for Education (DfE) (2013) *The National Curriculum in England: Key Stages 1 and 2.* London, DfE.

DfE (2014) *Statutory Framework for the Early Years Foundation Stage: Setting the Standards for Learning, Development and Care for Children from Birth to Five.* Available at: www.gov.uk/government/uploads/system/uploads/attachment_data/file/335504/EYFS_framework_from_1_September_2014__with_clarification_note.pdf (retrieved 21 November 2016).

Dillon, J. and Dickie, I. (2012) *Learning in the Natural Environment: Review of Social and Economic Benefits and Barriers.* Natural England Commissioned Reports, Number 092.

Fisher, J. (2010) *Moving on to Key Stage 1: Improving Transition from the Early Years Foundation Stage.* Maidenhead, OU Press.

Fisher, R. (2004) What is creativity? In Fisher, R. and Williams, M. (eds) *Unlocking Creativity: Teaching Across the Curriculum.* London, David Fulton.

Gibson, J. (1977) The theory of affordances. In Shaw, R. and Bransford, J. *Perceiving, Acting, and Knowing.* Hillsdale, N.J., Erlbaum.

Joyce, R. (2012) *Outdoor Learning: Past and Present.* Maidenhead, OU Press.

Kolb, D. A. (1984) *Experiential Learning: Experience as the Source of Learning and Development* (Vol. 1). Englewood Cliffs, NJ, Prentice-Hall.

Learning Through Landscapes (n.d.) *Getting Started: How Can We Get There?* Available at: www.ltl.org.uk/spaces/gettingstarted-3.php (retrieved 26 June 2016).

Lindon, J. (2011) *Too Safe for Their Own Good? Helping Children Learn about Risk and Life Skills.* London, National Children's Bureau.

Moffett, P. V. (2011) Outdoor mathematics trails: an evaluation of one training partnership. *Education 3–13: International Journal of Primary, Elementary and Early Years Education,* 39(3): 277–287.

Moylett, H. (2013) *Characteristics Of Effective Early Learning: Helping Young Children Become Learners For Life.* Maidenhead, OU Press.

NACCCE (National Advisory Committee on Creative and Cultural Education) (1999) *All Our Futures: Creativity, Culture and Education.* London, DfEE.

NAEYC (National Association for the Education of Young Children) (2009) *Developmentally Appropriate Practice in Early Childhood Programs Serving Children from Birth through Age 8.* Available at: www.naeyc.org/files/naeyc/file/positions/PSDAP.pdf (retrieved 20 January 2016).

National Trust (n.d.) *50 Things to Do Outdoors Before You're 11¾.* Available at: www.50things.org.uk/ (retrieved 20 June 2016).

Nutbrown, C. and Clough, P. (2014) *Early Childhood Education: History, Philosophy and Experience.* London, Sage.

Ofsted (2008) *Learning Outside the Classroom: How Far Should You Go?* London, HMSO.

Ouvrey, M (2003) *Exercising Muscles and Minds: Outdoor Play and the Early Years Curriculum.* London, National Children's Bureau.

Palmer, S. (2007) *Toxic Childhood: How The Modern World Is Damaging Our Children and What We Can Do About It.* London, Orion Books Ltd.

Rickinson, M., Dillon, J., Teamey, K., Morris, M., Choi, M. Y., Sanders, D. and Benefield, P. (2004) *A Review of Research on Outdoor Learning.* London, Field Studies Council.

Rickinson, M., Hunt, A., Rogers, J. and Dillon, J. (2012) *School Leader and Teacher Insights into Learning Outside the Classroom in Natural Environments.* Natural England Commissioned Reports, Number 097.

Sharp, C. (2006) *Making the Transition from Foundation Stage to Key Stage 1.* Presentation at the Early Years Conference, Skipton, 23 September.

Stephen, C. (2006) *Early Years Education: Perspectives from a Review of the International Literature.* Edinburgh, Scottish Executive Education Department.

Tovey, H. (2007) *Playing Outdoors: Spaces and Places, Risk and Challenge.* Maidenhead, OU Press.

UNESCO (2006) *Strong Foundations: Early Childhood Care and Education.* Paris, UNESCO.

Waite, S. (2010) Losing our way? The downward path for outdoor learning for children aged 2–11 years. *Journal of Adventure Education and Outdoor Learning*, 10(2), 111–126.

Waite, S., Evans, J. and Rogers, S. (2011) A time of change: outdoor learning and pedagogies of transition between Foundation Stage and Year 1. In Waite, S. *Children Learning Outside the Classroom: From Birth to Eleven.* London, Sage.

Whawell, G. and Tanner, J. (2015) Not like in the classroom! *Primary Geographer,* 88.

White, J. (2014) (2nd edn) *Playing and Learning Outdoors: Making Provision for High-quality Learning Experiences in the Outdoor Environment with Children 3–7.* London, Routledge.

Whitebread, D. (2012) *Developmental Psychology and Early Childhood Education.* London, Sage.

Wood, E. A. (2013) *Play, Learning and the Early Childhood Curriculum.* London, Sage.

STREETWORK

Investigating streets and buildings in the local area

Stephen Scoffham

INTRODUCTION

The streets and buildings in the immediate school vicinity are a potentially valuable teaching resource but are often overlooked. The differences between individual houses, the variety of architectural styles and the quality of the urban environment raise fascinating and far-reaching questions that relate to many areas of the curriculum. Children often appreciate local outdoor work because it values their surroundings and helps them to develop their sense of belonging. Furthermore, wherever your school may be, local streets and houses will be easy to access and can be studied on a regular basis. The opportunity to enrich the curriculum through 'streetwork' lies literally just across the doorstep. This chapter explores some of the possibilities and links them to deeper educational thinking on learning, pupil motivation and environmental awareness.

FIELDWORK, OUTDOOR LEARNING AND THE CURRICULUM

In recent years there has been renewed and sustained interest in outdoor work and the value of practical activities in the local environment have been increasingly acknowledged. On a policy level the *Learning Outside the Classroom Manifesto* (DfES 2006) represented a key government commitment which has been maintained despite subsequent curriculum changes. The growing enthusiasm for Forest Schools illustrates the appetite amongst teachers and children for practical activities in natural settings. Experiencing the rural environment and finding out about the plants and creatures in different locations is one way of developing environmental awareness. So too is work in urban settings.

There is increasingly strong evidence that exposure to nature and outdoor work brings health benefits and an improved sense of well-being. Malone (2008) concludes from a review of around 100 research papers from around the globe that outdoor learning can improve physical fitness, increase confidence and self-esteem, develop leadership qualities and promote leadership skills. A milestone report by the National Trust (Moss 2010) highlights the health, education, community and environmental benefits that result from interaction with the natural world. Ofsted (2008) have also affirmed that first hand experiences outside the classroom can 'contribute significantly to pupils' personal, social and emotional development' (p. 7).

Official support for fieldwork and outdoor learning is also embedded in the National Curriculum. In England, for example, children in KS1 are required to 'use simple fieldwork and observational skills' in geography, in science it is expected that 'most learning should be done through first hand practical experiences', while in design and technology children have to 'work in a range of relevant contexts' one of which is the local community (DfE 2013). In Scotland fieldwork is included in the social studies curriculum where the experiences and outcomes for infants include an expectation that children will 'explore places, investigate artefacts and locate them in time' (Education Scotland 2010). Similar requirements permeate the curricula of Wales and Northern Ireland and extend to the upper age bands in all four UK jurisdictions.

Fieldwork is often associated with residential study visits to rural areas. Thus children from London may undertake visits to locations in North Wales or the Lake District, where dramatic landscapes provide a stark contrast with the environments where the children live their daily lives. Such visits can be immensely stimulating and have significant educational impact. However, fieldwork has many other dimensions. It can be undertaken in both urban and rural locations and at a range of scales from the local to the distant. Studies that focus on local streets and buildings may not have the same initial appeal as residential study visits but they can be just as meaningful. And because they focus on environments that people have created co-operatively over many years they are imbued with strong social, cultural and aesthetic dimensions.

STREETWORK

Local studies that focus on streets and buildings – streetwork – is a distinctive form of fieldwork with particular qualities and pedagogies. The term 'streetwork' was first coined in the 1970s (see Ward and Fyson 1973) to express radical new ideas about schooling and the opportunities for young people to become active citizens engaged in creating and shaping urban communities – a vision which chimes with more recent thinking about children's voices and participatory initiatives in education. Returning to this concept nowadays has the advantage of capturing something of the original vision and passion of those who advocated alternative forms of education and who understood that communities, rather than being static, were characterised by dynamic and ever-changing interactions. Thus streetwork involves much more than simply describing and recording the features of the immediate environment, important though this is. It also suggests the idea that children, just as much as adults, have a role to play in creating balanced and healthy communities, are part of the social fabric and have views which deserve to be acknowledged and respected (Figure 3.1).

Such an approach resonates with modern thinking about places. On one level the built environment can be thought of in physical terms. Bricks and mortar are combined in different ways to make buildings; tarmac and paving stones establish the pattern of local streets. However, this visible framework has little to say about lived experiences. It is the way that people inhabit urban spaces and interact with each other on a daily basis that creates communities and brings the environment to life. Furthermore, just as buildings are continually wearing away and need to be updated, so the connections which people make

▨ **Figure 3.1** Children exploring and recording features in a local street
(Photo by Gemma Kent)

to each other and their surroundings are constantly changing and evolving. Massey (2005) has drawn attention to the social and cultural dimensions of place which she sees as nodes or intersections where different people and ideas cross at particular moments in time. Recognising that the environment is fluid rather than fixed and acknowledging that the way that we interpret our surroundings is also part of its fabric, focus attention on process rather than form and gives access to deeper levels of understanding.

Getting started

Having the confidence to use the local built environment as a teaching resource is not always easy. To begin with it is often difficult to find out any detailed information about a specific locality. Guide books and historical accounts may provide a few clues, old maps will reveal changes in settlement patterns and local council planning documents and environmental appraisals can be informative but the coverage will almost invariably be fragmented. Census data is liable to be more comprehensive and can prove invaluable but tends to involve more detailed research and investigation. It is best to recognise from the outset that the suburban settings where many primary schools are located are likely to be poorly documented. But then streetwork is only tangentially concerned with factual knowledge. It is much more to do with open ended exploration and investigation – about putting pupils at the centre of learning and giving them the chance to engage with their surroundings on their own terms in ways which relate to their level of understanding.

Whatever the nature of your locality, careful planning is an essential part of outdoor work. Exploring on foot is one of the best ways to identify different features of the local environment and to assess its streetwork potential. Some houses may be built against the pavement making it possible for children to study the front doors. Others may have front gardens that are either partially or completely paved, suggesting an interesting comparative land use study. There may be vacant plots and wasteland sites which are earmarked for redevelopment which pupils can assess and investigate. Cul de sacs make a safe working environment with clear boundaries and little traffic.

It is important to recognise that taking children out of doors involves a break in routine and requires different working practices. Some children find the experience both exciting and disturbing and behave accordingly. If your class becomes a little unruly on their first outing don't take this as a sign of failure. The novelty of the initial visit soon wears off as pupils come to realise that learning can happen in different places in different ways. Excitement is a sign of enthusiasm.

One of the other barriers to streetwork concerns health and safety issues. The welfare of children is every teacher's paramount concern and it is vital to complete a risk assessment. Schools will have their own guidelines indicating minimum levels of adult supervision and established health and safety procedures for fieldwork. Parental consent will need to be obtained and procedures put in place in the unlikely event of emergencies. These requirements, which can be onerous for a single study visit, become much less burdensome when streetwork is undertaken on a regular basis and is seen as part of the established curriculum. Any risk assessment and documentation can then apply to multiple, rather than individual, outings.

SUGGESTIONS FOR TEACHING AND LEARNING

The ideas presented in the following section outline a range of possible streetwork activities for children aged 5–11. They are intended to whet the appetite rather than to be comprehensive. Much will depend on the nature of the locality and the enthusiasms and interests of both yourself and the pupils that you teach. As a general principle, you might like to give the pupils a simple outline map of the local streets so they can follow where they go while they are working out of doors. Marking different routes and adding significant information week by week is a valuable way of developing mapwork skills. There is also much to be said for giving each child their own personal streetwork sketchbook. This will provide a single place where they can make drawings, record data and devise diagrams. Additionally, the sketchbook will serve to distinguish streetwork from more everyday classroom activities and help to boost its status. You might also want to think about how to organise any photographs. A single class site for streetwork images will allow pupils to pool their photographs and give the entire class an increasingly comprehensive archive which they can use according to their needs.

Thinking about streets and buildings

You can start thinking about local streets and buildings even before you leave the classroom. One particularly engaging approach is to use a picture book which is either set in an urban environment or which describes a particular house or set of buildings. Greek and Roman myths often refer to ancient cities; many classic fairy tales have illustrations of historic houses. When it comes to contemporary settings, two wordless books for older readers by Jeannie Baker are particularly noteworthy. *Window* (Baker 2002) shows how the same scene framed by a window gradually changes as the boy who gazes through it grows older with the passing years. The loss of trees, the growth in housing and increasing urbanisation provide rich topics for discussion. A companion story, *Belonging* (Baker 2008), takes a reverse perspective and depicts the way in which an urban setting can be transformed by environmental initiatives. As well as stimulating conversations about the environment, these two books are, as Dolan (2014) notes, valuable ways to help children think about community, family and relationships. As such they serve to demonstrate complex concepts such as interaction and interdependence in a meaningful way.

Houses and homes

Houses and homes are perhaps one of the most immediate and accessible streetwork topics. Children's innate desire for security and their personal experience of growing up have always made this a popular area of study with infants. Animal homes such as insect burrows, bird nests and the homes for household pets provide an engaging entry point but the chance to find out about actual houses in the immediate school locality takes this study to a new level. Children are also quick to pick up on the way streetwork attributes value to the places where they live, particularly if their own home becomes the object of study. Be careful, though, as it is all too easy to start making judgements (both positive and negative) which could easily have unfortunate implications.

ACTIVITY BOX **FRONT DOORS**

Young children might begin by making a survey of front door colours. It is possible to start this survey in the classroom by asking the children about the colour of their own front door but a street survey will make the study more immediate and meaningful and provoke discussions about how we describe different colours and how we respond to them. Record the findings on a block graph before extending the work. There are lots of questions to investigate. How many doors have porches or places to shelter? Are the bell and letter box easy to reach? Is there a door knocker? Does the doorway seem welcoming? Get the children to make annotated drawings in their streetwork sketch books. You might extend the work back at school by getting pupils to make a drawing of their own front door. Cut round the three moving edges of the door, fold back the fourth to make it 'open' and double mount it on a second sheet of paper. Pupils can then write a few sentences about themselves and their family in the area behind the door for a class 'community' display. If you leave the doors 'closed' viewers will be able to open each one in turn to find out what lies behind.

ACTIVITY BOX **WALLS AND ROOFS**

There are two main families or types of wall. Frame walls use wooden or metal beams to transfer the weight of the roof to the ground. This means that the windows can be set in the gaps and have no impact on the strength of the structure. Solid walls (which are often made of brick or concrete blocks) are an unbroken mass which gives the wall considerable strength but means it is weakened by doors, windows and other openings. Traditionally houses were built of local materials but with the Industrial Revolution and the coming of the railways in the mid nineteenth century it suddenly became possible to carry heavy building materials large distances. Across large parts of Britain houses were erected using Welsh slates and Midland bricks. Nowadays, glass, metal and plastic are increasingly widely used, although often disguised to look like their traditional counterparts. Investigating and recording the materials used in local buildings can be the start of a much wider topic on resources and structures. Look for examples of solid and frame walling and make house models for a display (Figure 3.2). Decide whether the roof is hipped (same height on all sides) or pitched (carried up the main ridge on two sides only). Collect a range of building materials such as wood, brick, tile and slate for the children to handle. Talk about their properties so famously explored in the tale of the 'Three Little Pigs'. Think about how different materials decay and need to be protected. Look at the way water is carried from the roof down the walls and into the gutter. This forms part of the water cycle and illustrates one small section of the passage of water from clouds in the atmosphere to rivers and seas on the ground. Challenge the children to construct diagrams to show aspects of the water cycle in your area naming any local streams, rivers, lakes and marshes.

■ **Figure 3.2** Model houses with roofs of slate and tile arranged as a street pattern by Key Stage 1 children

(Photo by Stephen Scoffham)

ACTIVITY BOX **PERSONALISATION**

People personalise their houses in different ways. Small stone carvings of animals are commonly found around gates and entrances but also feature as garden ornaments. The number or name of the house is often written in distinctive ways, sometimes on a decorated tile or as ornate metalwork. There are notices which either welcome visitors or tell them to 'Beware of the Dog'. Sometimes a blank wall is decorated with a mural or simply used to display plants in hanging baskets. Making a record of different local examples, using either sketches, words or photographs, could form the basis of a class guide. Extend the study by getting pupils to devise a walk round the local area based on their favourite decorations. Younger pupils might simply concentrate on patterns and shapes. Finding different examples of squares, triangles, rectangles and instances of tessellating patterns as in mosaic paths and tilework is a valuable way of consolidating classroom work in mathematics and art. This might also be something to share with a partner school as part of a portrait of your locality.

ACTIVITY BOX **IDEAL HOME**

Get the children to design an ideal or imaginary home, drawing on ideas they have gleaned from their streetwork studies. One device which works particularly well is to give groups of children a household object such as a milk jug, cheese grater or colander to use as a frame for their design. Challenge the children to position the window and doors within the spaces available. This might then lead into thinking about the design of individual rooms and the internal layout. There are also natural links to stories and poems. For example, can pupils come up with an illustration to go with the rhyme about the old woman who lived in a shoe with all her children? An entirely different way of developing the work is to get the children to identify what they think are the 'best' buildings in their neighbourhood. Developing the criteria by which to make a judgement is likely to prompt a wide-ranging discussion and include issues to do with sustainability as well as design.

Exploring local streets

Many of the children in your class will be familiar with the immediate environment. They will know the best places to play ball games, where they can go to build dens, various hiding and secret places, the different routes they can use as short cuts. One of the most comprehensive and sensitive studies of children's use of the local surroundings (Hart 1979) noted the extraordinary resourcefulness and intelligence with which children transformed their environment. This led Hart to conclude that schools need to give fuller recognition to environmental competence and the creativity involved in it. The streetwork activities suggested below have the potential to support and develop this kind of initiative.

ACTIVITY BOX **EXPLORATION CARDS**

Start with a game! Get the children to make a set of around 12 exploration cards with different instructions. As well as including directions for orienteering (turn left/right, go forward/take ten steps back) the cards might challenge the players to find different items such as a traffic sign, a garden with a hedge, or a litter bin. It can be fun to pretend so get the children to imagine different scenarios. 'You're going on a journey so you need to find a bus stop.' 'You're a painter or builder looking for a house which needs repair.' 'You're a fireman looking for a fire hydrant in an emergency.' Once they have made the cards (and you have vetted them) get the children to play the game in pairs in a safe local street, taking the cards in turn and following the instructions if possible. An alternative would be to create a 'mystery tour' in which a pair of children devise a set of directions linking some interesting places for another pair to follow.

ACTIVITY BOX **STREET FURNITURE**

The different items which people add to a street to serve their needs are known as street furniture (Figure 3.3). Make a survey of local street furniture using tally marks. Are there any items which are no longer needed and have been left over from the past? What things are missing or might improve the street? Do any of the existing items need to be repaired?

■ **Figure 3.3** There is a considerable variety of street furniture in every city side street (Photo by Stephen Scoffham)

ACTIVITY BOX **TRAPS AND COVERS**

In most areas there are large numbers of traps and covers set into the pavement. These give access to essential services buried underground including water and gas pipes, electric and fibre optic cables, rain water and other sewers. Finding out about these different services helps children to understand the infra-structure which supports modern life. It also illustrates the impact we have on the environment both in terms of the resources we consume (inputs) and the waste we create (outputs). Use large sheets of paper and wax crayons to make rubbings of any metal covers you can find. These will make an engaging wall display and could stimulate further work on patterns and design. A word of warning! When undertaking this exercise remember that traps and covers are also found in the middle of the road and have to be strictly out of bounds for safety reasons.

ACTIVITY BOX **SUSTAINABLE STREET SURVEY**

Make a survey of local streets focusing on sustainability or environmental issues. Can pupils find any water meters, recycling bins, solar panels or other clues that people are trying to reduce their environmental impact? How are people trying to support wildlife? Many houses have bird feeders and bird boxes in their front gardens. Some gardens are stocked with flowers which are particularly attractive to bees and butterflies. Providing creatures with water is also important so children need to see if they can find any ponds in their vicinity. A study of trees and plants is another possibility. What different species can pupils find in and around their school? Do they look healthy and what benefits do they bring? Are there any places where new trees could be planted to improve the local environment? If so, what species would you choose?

ACTIVITY BOX **TOWNSCAPES**

The term 'townscape' refers to the visual quality of the built environment and is the urban equivalent of landscape. Make a study of the local streets and buildings using sketches and photographs to record significant townscape features. Some key terms such as framing, linking, screening, silhouette, intricacy, texture and immediacy are illustrated and explained in Figure 3.4. Once pupils have grasped these ideas they will start finding examples throughout the neighbourhood. Developing a townscape vocabulary can be a source of lasting pleasure as it sharpens our perception of the structures and spaces in towns and cities. It also enables us to critically appraise the built environment and thus provides the touchstone for suggesting changes and improvements. As the Commission for Architecture and the Built Environment (CABE) put it, 'visual awareness is more than just "looking"; it is also about "seeing", and seeing leads to understanding' (2007, p. 5).

TOWNSCAPE FEATURES

Here and there The division of space by a barrier or obstacle.		**Framing** A porch, archway or gap which traps a distant view.	
Enclosure Spaces which are shut in or covered with a roof.		**Linking** Devices which link places, a bit like joining words in a sentence.	
Punctuation A broken view or visual pause, rather like a comma in a sentence.		**Silhouette** The outline of buildings against the sky.	
Focal point A statue, column or spire which attracts attention. A full stop.		**Intricacy** A complicated visual outline. A kind of puzzle.	
Mystery A partly hidden view which creates a sense of anticipation.		**Texture** The quality of a surface – smooth, hard, rough and so on.	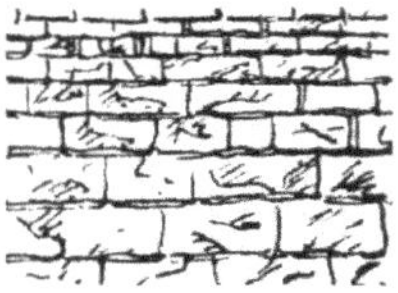
Repetition A regular pattern of windows, chimneys, doors and decorations.		**Exposure** Bleak, unprotected spaces which are open to wind, sun and rain.	
Surprise Something which is unexpected, humorous or shocking.		**Sunken area** A cosy, sheltered spot where people are happy to linger.	
Screening A wall or building which is partly hidden by plants or trees.		**High point** The top of a hill or tower which looks out over other places.	

Figure 3.4 Developing the language and vocabulary to describe the built environment helps children to develop their thinking

---

ACTIVITY BOX **NEW DESIGNS**

Wherever you live there are likely to be open spaces which for some reason have either been abandoned or which are awaiting redevelopment. These provide an ideal opportunity for pupils to come up with their own plans and suggestions. Begin by making a survey of the site, identifying different entry points and sight lines to surrounding buildings. A good plan will be essential. The next stage is to discuss possible uses and to consider the scale and scope of any new buildings, perhaps using models. Once pupils have devised more detailed proposals and visualisations they might present their ideas to other groups and classes. Some schools invite local planners and architects to act as advisers and critics. Others ask local councillors to explain the local authority's plans. Such engagements not only raise the status of the work. They are also a way of building community links and contributing to making local decisions – children are surprisingly good at asking penetrating questions which can even take professionals by surprise.

REFLECTIONS ON STREETWORK

It will be apparent from the range of activities suggested above that streetwork can be extremely varied, that it can be pitched in different ways according to the age and ability of the pupils and that it has the potential to enrich and invigorate the curriculum. It is also supported by a distinctive pedagogy and ethos which recognises the importance of exploration and enquiry and gives children the opportunity to follow their interests and enthusiasms. Such an approach respects the integrity of the child and provides spaces and contexts where their creativity can flourish. There are a number of key features.

Streetwork involves active learning

Pedagogically, streetwork involves active learning. Teachers can devise structures and help to focus pupils' attention but the way they respond is crucial. The richness and diversity of local streets and buildings means that there are multiple entry points to learning and opportunities to pursue different lines of enquiry. There are also natural opportunities to use a range of recording techniques and different methods of analysis. Crucially there is no set body of knowledge to be communicated. Rather, pupils apply the skills they have learnt in the classroom as they explore their surroundings and reflect on their findings through discussion and analysis. As a result, the built environment serves as a text which children can 'read' in lots of different ways.

Streetwork harnesses children's curiosity and personal knowledge

We are naturally curious about the world and have a deep-seated urge to explore our surroundings. By helping children find out about their local streets and buildings, streetwork taps into one of the basic forces which drive human behaviour. Witt (2017) argues that placing children at the heart of learning enables them to draw on their personal experiences to enhance their knowledge and understanding. Asking questions and imagining alternatives is part of a playful approach which generates spaces for creative thinking.

Furthermore, Claxton (1998) argues that 'slow' or playful learning allows us to access deeper levels of thought, as opposed to more 'deliberate' modes which operate on a surface level to generate quick decisions. These approaches are best seen as complementary rather than exclusive, just as systematic streetwork surveys can be set alongside open-ended questions and speculation.

Streetwork is memorable and enjoyable

Many children enjoy streetwork and welcome the chance to work out of doors. 'It was wonderful to be out of doors once in my life,' a child once remarked on her return from a streetwork outing. Her comment was significant because when we find things enjoyable learning becomes easier and we are disposed to find out more. Research by Nundy (1999) has identified the positive, cognitive and affective benefits of outdoor work in rural areas with upper juniors. One of Nundy's arguments is that 'key memory episodes' derived from experience serve as reference points which facilitate learning. It seems likely that streetwork provides similar memorable experiences. A survey of 2000 adolescents by CABE (2010), for example, found that nine out of ten pupils said they remembered 'more from a school outing than from a class lesson' (p. 2). When we are working out of doors we are actively involved and all our senses are mobilised.

Streetwork empowers children

Undertaking enquiries and asking questions are a central part of streetwork and serve to engage children with their environment. Thus the studies which they undertake serve not only to boost their emotional engagement with their immediate surroundings, they also open up discussions about possible changes and developments (Figure 3.5). Discussing improvements is not always positive – it implies a deficit model and that improvements need to be made. Thinking of yourself as an active agent, however, and recognising that you have the power to make changes is fundamentally affirmative as it serves to boost confidence and self-image.

Streetwork changes teacher/pupil relations

Working out of doors and studying local streets and buildings impacts on teacher/pupil relations. The power relations which operate in the classroom tend to be broken down in outdoor environments to be replaced by more collaborative and participatory structures. There are also better opportunities for teachers and pupils to converse on a more equal footing and share ideas and information. The sense that everyone is working together gives children greater authority – there are opportunities for them to become 'experts' and their local knowledge means they may well know more than their teacher.

Streetwork strengthens community links

Streetwork activities serve to build children's understanding of the community. They may be finding out the history of the area and the people who shaped it in the past. They may be thinking about the future and how the area is changing. They may be investigating local facilities or recording the features which contribute to its identity. Booth and Ainscrow

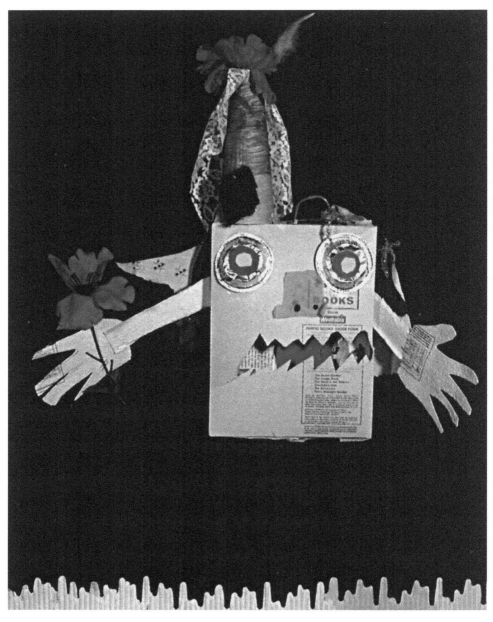

Figure 3.5 A design for a litter bin that people would want to use, proposed by a Year 3 child (Photo by Stephen Scoffham)

(2010) see learning about local facilities in the vicinity of the school as one of the indicators of inclusive practice. Meanwhile, Alexander (2010), in his extensive review of primary education, found that children wanted schools to engage with 'real life issues' and not limit themselves to 'inward-looking agendas' (p. 65). Many adults would echo these sentiments.

Streetwork brings subjects together in cross-curricular studies

Streetwork provides an opportunity to develop work in all subject areas. Some studies will have a strong discipline focus, i.e. finding out about decorations in art or writing street poems in English. However, combining subjects in different ways often emerges as a natural way of learning when it comes to outdoor work. Barnes (2015, p. 1) makes the point that 'everything that surrounds us in the physical world can be seen and understood from multiple perspectives'. He also reminds us that 'our experience of the world is cross-curricular'. Building on real world interactions is a central part of streetwork. And if we are to honour pupil rather than adult perspectives we need to avoid compartmentalising experiences into subject silos.

Streetwork attributes value to the local area

When they undertake streetwork, children are using the area where they live as a learning resource. This can be highly affirmative. Just as positive role models play a significant part in supporting behavioural norms, so focusing on the local area implies that the local environment is to be valued and treasured. There are also plenty of opportunities for children to consolidate and reinforce their learning. The study of front doors, for example, which pupils may have conducted as a streetwork activity, can be applied and extended as they make their way back home at the end of the day.

Streetwork supports pro-environmental behaviours

There is growing evidence that exposure to the natural environment in childhood provides the foundation for environmental concern in later life (Louv 2008; Sobel 2008; Kellert 2009). By the same token it is reasonable to suppose that those who engage with the built environment in their youth will be more likely to value their surroundings in adulthood. Barnes (2013, p. 24) provides support for this way of thinking. He contends that the enhanced environmental sensitivity that follows from local environmental work 'often spawns concern for sustainable, more inclusive futures'. The dangers of rearing children in what have been called 'battery-reared conditions' are all too apparent.

Streetwork can enhance global understanding

The benefits that accrue from investigating the local area are not restricted simply to local knowledge. If pupils have a detailed understanding of their own environment it can provide them with a template for understanding other, more distant, places and cultures. This relates directly to work on British values. Many UK schools now have links with partner schools overseas. Compiling a portrait of their own locality and communicating it to pupils in another country gives streetwork additional relevance. At the same time, UK children who have explored their own locality will be better able to interpret information about other places.

CONCLUSION

At its finest the built environment is one of humanity's greatest achievements. It represents an extraordinary collective endeavour which draws on ideas from science, art and technology and other subjects to express a range of human aspirations and beliefs. The values which permeate different cultures and societies are made manifest in the buildings and cities they create. The humble, everyday surroundings in which most of us live our lives make no such claims but are nevertheless cultural and social artefacts which children can engage with as part of their upbringing and from which they can discover a great deal. Learning to 'read' the built environment and to critically appraise its various qualities can be a source of life-long pleasure as well as part of what it means to be an educated citizen.

In Britain today around 80 per cent of people live in towns and cities and an even higher proportion of children are educated in urban areas. It is therefore rather surprising that the educational potential of the built environment is so often overlooked. The diversity and richness of the natural world is undoubtedly a factor. Yet on one level at least there is nothing unnatural about streets and buildings. They may have been created by people but people take their place alongside other creatures as part of the life of the planet.

Streetwork has fallen out of fashion – a casualty perhaps of an increasingly narrow curriculum and growing fears about health and safety. Yet, as Peter Smith, one time president of the National Association of Field Studies Officers, contends, children have an entitlement to local off-site learning which can and should be retained (2014). This entitlement has a number of dimensions and requires a good knowledge of different teaching techniques if it is to be fully realised. Indeed, the capacity, capability and confidence of teachers and teachers in training are paramount. Local streets and buildings are an immensely valuable free teaching resource which is literally on the doorstep. Unlike trips and visits to more distant places, there are no costs to negotiate or complicated travel arrangements to organise. Every child and every teacher in every classroom in the country can access the built environment. For this reason alone we ought to be using it better.

REFERENCES

Alexander, R. (2010) *Children, Their World, Their Education*, London: Routledge.

Baker, J. (2002) *Window*, London: Walker Books.

Baker, J. (2008) *Belonging*, London: Walker Books.

Barnes, J. (2013) 'Can We Use the Built Environment to Support Children's Learning?' in Sangster, M. (Ed) *Developing Teacher Expertise*, London: Bloomsbury.

Barnes, J. (2015) *Cross-curricular Learning 3–14*, (3rd edn), London: Sage.

Barnes, J. (2014) *Cross-Curricular Learning 3–14*, London: Sage.

Booth, T. and Ainscrow, M. (2010) (3rd edn) *Index for Inclusion: Developing Learning and Participation in Schools*, Bristol: Centre for Studies on Inclusive Education.

CABE (Commission for Architecture and the Built Environment) (2007) *Our Street: Learning to See*, London: CABE.

CABE (Commission for Architecture and the Built Environment) (2010) *Unforgettable Lessons: An Introduction to Engaging Places,* London: CABE.

Claxton, G. (1998) *Hare Brain, Tortoise Mind*, London: Fourth Estate.

DfE (2013) *National Curriculum in England: Primary Curriculum*. Available at www.gov.uk/government/collections/national-curriculum (accessed 18 November 2016).

DfES (2006) *Learning Outside the Classroom Manifesto*, Nottingham: DfES. Available at www.lotc.org.uk/wp-content/uploads/2011/03/G1.-LOtC-Manifesto.pdf (accessed 18 November 2016).

Dolan, A. (2014) *You, Me and Diversity*, London: Institute of Education.

Education Scotland (2010) *Curriculum for Excellence*. Available at www.educationscotland.gov.uk/learningandteaching/thecurriculum/ (accessed 18 November 2016).

Hart, R. (1979) *Children's Experience of Place*, New York: Irvington.

Kellert, S. (2009) 'A Biocultural Basis for an Environmental Ethic' in Kellert, S. and Speth, G. (eds) *The Coming Transformation*, Yale: Yale School of Forestry and Environmental Studies.

Louv, R. (2008) *Last Child in the Woods*, Chapel Hill, North Carolina: Algonquin.

Malone, K. (2008) *Every Experience Matters*, Report commissioned by Farming and Countryside Education for UK Department Children, School and Families, Wollongong, Australia.

Massey, D. (2005) *For Space*, London: Sage.

Moss. S. (2010) *Natural Childhood*. Available at www.nationaltrust.org.uk/documents/read-our-natural-childhood-report.pdf (accessed 18 November 2016).

Nundy, S. (1999) 'The Fieldwork Effect: The Role and Impact of Fieldwork in the Upper Primary School', *International Research in Geographical and Environmental Education*, 8.2, 190–198.

Ofsted (2008) *Learning Outside the Classroom*, London: Ofsted.

Smith, P. (2014) 'A President's View 2013', *NAFSO Journal 2013–2014*, 37.

Sobel, D. (2008) *Childhood and Nature: Design Principles for Educators*, Portland, Maine: Stenhouse.

Ward, C. and Fyson, T. (1973) *Streetwork: The Exploding School*, London: Routledge and Kegan Paul.

Witt, S. (2017) 'Playful Approaches to Learning Out of Doors' in Scoffham, S. (ed., 2nd edn.) *Teaching Geography Creatively*, London: Routledge.

Websites

Council for Learning Outside the Classroom www.lotc.org.uk/

Engaging Places www.engagingplaces.org.uk/home

CHAPTER 4

CREATIVE FIELDWORK
Whose place is this anyway?

Paula Owens

INTRODUCTION

Fieldwork through participative enquiry begs creative and critical approaches that genuinely involve pupils of all ages. Whether in the school grounds, the immediate or wider locality, children from Reception upwards ought to have opportunities to creatively re-imagine possibilities for both stewardship and change in their environment and to effect appropriate actions. This chapter sets out a rationale for creative fieldwork by arguing for the importance of a reliable framework built around key concepts and different ways of knowing.

THE EARTH BELONGS TO ALL OF US!

In a well-known children's storybook, Michael Foreman's *Dinosaurs and All That Rubbish* (1993), humans have over-exploited the Earth's resources and it is down to sleeping dinosaurs to awaken and save the world from pollution, deforestation and the general destruction of natural habitats. 'The Earth belongs to all of us!' (Foreman 1993) is a powerful, last refrain as the humans in the story experience a seismic shift in their awareness and realise how selfish they have been.

The Earth does belong to all of us, humans and other living beings, as we belong to it. We all co-exist interdependently through, and often despite, our individual and collective resource demands. Yet it is an unhappy fact that the Earth belongs to some more than others and that contested spaces exist between humans, between other species and between humans and other species. A discernible, complex web of interactions between human and physical environments and processes leaves marks on the planet and is further complicated by a less visible but equally complex moral web of collective and individual rights, responsibilities and obligations that is in a state of constant flux.

Michael Foreman's book, *Dinosaurs and All That Rubbish*, provoked much work on environmentalism in the 1990s: it was an era when attendant work through organisations such as 'Eco-Schools' flourished as schools gained confidence in their 'green' credentials. From litter picking to composting, careful energy use to healthy meals and traffic surveys to pond clearances, schools embraced notions of sustainability. But the world has changed dramatically since then: development of, and access to, the internet and virtual learning has developed so much that today most children in the UK and other more developed countries will have access to mobile phones, online gaming platforms and, of course, laptops and tablets. In addition, there is a greater perceived risk for children to roam free out of doors whilst the twin pressure of increased development has reduced physical access to the local area.

Today children in the so-called 'modern world' are said to be suffering what has been termed a 'nature deficit' (Louv 2013) as they live lives increasingly alienated from nature. However, arguably the problem is deeper than that as it is not just natural environments that children today are experiencing less of; they are spending less time in any kind of outdoor environment. It is well documented that children spend less time out of doors than in the past due to a variety of reasons (Pretty et al. 2009). Today's children in the more developed global North are likely to be learning about the world through mediated rather than first-hand experiences.

Here we are, in the 21st century and the world is in even more desperate need of creative thinkers who can solve a host of problems that at best threaten quality of life and, at worst, threaten our very existence. We need thinkers and doers for the future who can navigate outdoor and real landscapes and make reasoned, informed judgements. If this is an area that children are becoming ever more unfamiliar with it is even more important that education helps to redress this imbalance.

FIELDWORK MATTERS

Fieldwork and outdoor learning offer powerful and inimitable opportunities to engage in the real world beyond the classroom, where processes do not always follow textbook rules and theoretical underpinnings. The real world is complex, messy and unpredictable, with implications for geographical and wider understanding (Pickering 2017), but it is also exciting, scary and a source of wonder and of despair. All this is powerful grist for education.

Real world knowledge, and its attendant issues and problems, are a fertile and necessary ground for the geographer, satisfying what Lambert and Reiss (2014) describe as the subject's 'commitment to exploration and enquiry, and its concern to discover and to be curious about the world' (p. 8). Indeed, there is a strong argument to be made for the inclusion of such a statement within every primary subject. Considerable evidence from research points to the wide-ranging educational benefits of fieldwork enquiry in teaching and learning science, for example (ASE 2011), and further examples litter the curricula. Although schools may interpret outdoor learning in various ways there is common agreement as to the benefits to pupils of taking learning outside of the classroom (Rickinson et al. 2012). As both current and future decision-makers, which is what we all are, we need to be well informed and able to see the bigger picture. Creative problem-solving, through real-world engagement and outdoor learning, serves a most vital part of education, providing hope and vision for better futures (Hicks 2014).

Fieldwork matters for many reasons. It is a statutory part of the geography curriculum and thus of the England National Curriculum (DfE 2014). More than that, it is recognised as an essential aspect of the subject across all curricula (GA 2009). In a wider education context, the 'Global Goals' are a set of aims for strategic action intended to succeed the Millennium Development Goals (MDGs) post 2015 and deepen a case for the core importance of education in identifying and creating better futures (UN 2015). Some lasting principles with 'universal relevance' were identified in a UNESCO (2014) report as those that ought to guide education policy post 2015. One of these is given below:

> Education is a foundation for human fulfilment, peace, sustainable development, economic growth, decent work, gender equality and responsible global citizenship . . . In addition to the acquisition of basic knowledge and cognitive skills, the content of learning must promote problem solving and creative thinking.
>
> (UNESCO 2014, p. 3)

Sustainable development and global citizenship are real life issues requiring a focus and immersion in the real world through problem-solving activities, enquiry-led learning, analysis and action. Fieldwork offers the opportunity to help meet some of these wider and worthy education aims that look towards sustainable futures. It is also vital in providing some support for children to experience and interpret the real world with a view to becoming careful and thoughtful participants in their own environment and thus in the wider world.

Research has shown how positive, early, outdoor experiences are formative and may lead to the development of pro-environmental actions and thinking in later life (Catling et al. 2010). Children today live within vastly different concepts of time and space than they did in the past. The arrival of mass communication and media imposition has radically altered the essence of children's lives. Stables (1998) explored the concept of proximity and distance in relation to moral behaviours and posited that children today were exposed to a rapid stream of real and virtual experiences, which included possible psychologically and emotionally disturbing aspects. Because of such bombardment, Stables (1998) suggested that children were unable to take the time to reflect on their attitudes towards the many more moral dilemmas that faced them and neither did they have the inclination to do so.

Purposeful fieldwork provides more opportunities for children to experience and learn about a local area that they may not always be that familiar with; creating significant and lasting memories and affective bonds in the process; and equipping them to better understand how they can act to improve it and sustain it. As such an important area within the context of education and sustainable futures, it is ever more important that fieldwork learning experiences are carefully crafted to maximise creative and purposeful learning.

FRAMING FIELDWORK

Fieldwork can happen in a wide range of settings with many guises: it can be playful, casual, open or structured and scientific. When fieldwork is both rigorous and creative, it has purposeful contexts framed by critical thinking and active decision-making. Creativity does not happen in a knowledge vacuum; it is fuelled by wide-ranging knowledge gathering and analysis that allows learners to be critical and focused as well as open and enquiring (Owens 2013).

ESSENTIAL CONCEPTS FOR GEOGRAPHY BASED FIELDWORK

In geography, any rigorous fieldwork ought to take account of three underpinning concepts: 'space' (or 'location'), 'place' and 'scale' (see Figure 4.1). Together these act as enquiry

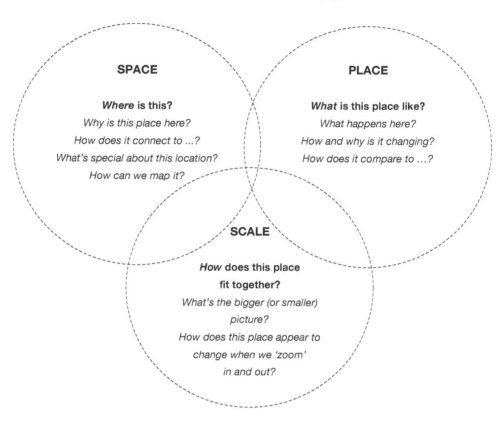

SPACE

Where is this?

Why is this place here?

How does it connect to ...?

What's special about this location?

How can we map it?

PLACE

What is this place like?

What happens here?

How and why is it changing?

How does it compare to ...?

SCALE

How does this place
fit together?

What's the bigger (or smaller)
picture?

How does this place appear to
change when we 'zoom'
in and out?

■ **Figure 4.1** Fieldwork: underpinning geographical concepts and questions

prompts to take account of local and global influences and the importance of location. The latter is especially important as, whilst a place might be described in great detail as to the features and characteristics it possesses, an enquiry only becomes geographical when a spatial component is added and then used to help identify and explain.

SPACE

Space and spatiality are often placed at the heart of geography and help to unify its many diverse aspects (Merriman et al. 2012). Although an abstract concept, space can be mapped in precise ways. At a mathematical level, space can be both measured and used as a marker to show whereabouts a location is in absolute terms. It can also be referred to in relative terms. As well as the non-negotiable facts about location like a specific position on the Earth's surface, the 'where' of places can be described in political and perceptual descriptors that are less certain.

Where is a place in terms of its geographical boundaries? Is it near a busy road, by the sea, in a dangerous part of town? Such descriptions differ from the absolute and the certain such as that provided by a map's grid reference, a post code or longitude and latitude and remind us that places have factual and perceptual qualities. Using spatial reference points are important in fieldwork as they help explain not just where a place is but what it is like: its attributes, issues and problems.

Location matters and can help explain why things are as they are, how they are changing and why and, often, why borders and places are contested. Even at the local scale of the playground, children will know that some places get too hot in the sun, other areas might have shady seats, some places are best for playing games, whilst others might be noisier as they are near a road. At a global scale, we know that the location of places relative to the poles and equator determine factors such as daylight length and climate and that proximity to certain phenomena, such as the meeting of tectonic plates, indicates increased risk to people living there.

SCALE

Ingold (2011) rails against the use of 'space' as he says it is too abstract, arguing that we do not live our lives inside places but rather in the spaces and connections between them, constantly in motion through a process he refers to as 'wayfaring'. If, he argues, wayfaring is a notion of paths or lines of motion along which we are continually travelling, then places are like knots signifying the enmeshing of lives where paths entwine (Ingold 2011). In a similar way, the concept of scale engulfs our everyday lives and wider imagined worlds as we move from home to school to the local area, to the region, country and global scale in no particular order and through a mix of first-hand and mediated experiences. Changes in scale are neither clearly definable nor hierarchical but rather a piece of a wider puzzle having both distinct and general characteristics.

When we refer to 'London' for example, we may refer to generalisations that draw on our knowledge of the capital but which would be out of place when describing a particular street in a part of London like, for example, Bermondsey. Yet Bermondsey owes its own distinctive make-up to its heritage within London and its connections to other locales within the region as well as places beyond. Fieldwork in any locale requires an understanding of context as to the 'where' a place is and how it connects to other places (space). Scale is a concept which prompts and encourages such thinking.

A local town may be described in terms of its 'town-ness' yet at a deeper level, there will be contrasting areas and contradictions that are only uncovered when 'zooming in' to take a close look. Anomalies can be present in a single street. 'Zooming out' from a town also helps uncover more information about the nature of a place e.g. who lives on the suburbs and why? How well connected is this place? Where does it connect to and why? What are the implications of its wider setting or its particular aspects? Teaching children to look for clues in locality fieldwork prompted by the notion of scale is another valuable tool for investigating 'place'.

PLACE

Space becomes 'place' according to Tuan (1977) when given meaning and increasingly so when imbued with values: what we might be able to or can do in a place defines it in both shared and personal ways. Places have names that are commonly accepted in everyday parlance and formal use although names also signify power relating to combinations of ownership, sovereignty or interest. Think of 'Mount Everest', a name give to the world's highest mountain by the British but which has many other identities. The Nepalese refer to Everest as *Sagarmatha*, loosely translated as the brow of the sky, and the Tibetan name for it is *Chomolungma*, which has been described as the look of a big, fluffy white hen! Each name has its own history, interpretation and offers different values and meanings to the place for the people who refer to it.

Place names often help describe the nature of a place, for example many places in Wales are preceded by 'Aber' or bridge followed by the name of a river, such as Aberystwyth. Names can, like location, be both factual and subjective and hold potent clues about the nature and ownership of a place (Relph 2015). Places also have reputations, some to the point of stereotypical association, and these can be powerful and enduring, entrenched even into a particular culture: for example, the 'poetic' Lake District or the 'terrorist stronghold' of Raqqua (also known as Al Raqqah or Rakka). Place names conjure up both shared and personal impressions in conveying a sense of what a place is like.

The affordance of place was a term coined by Gibson (1979) to explain how landscapes offer potential in terms of what might be done there. Tuan (1977) believed that while to an adult a place may hold deeply signified meanings and sentiments, a child will often dwell on the potential for movement that is implied by a place, as their imagination is tied to activity.

In an early yet seminal study of children in their local environment, Hart (1978) observed how children gave names to places reflecting what they could do there and how they would use a 'short cut', which was in fact longer, because it was more exciting to travel through i.e. the potential offered by the route was more important than merely getting there. However, Hart (2015) concluded, after replicating some of this early, groundbreaking (1978) work with children some thirty years later, that children's range and autonomy as well as their knowledge of 'secret places' has diminished considerably and that time is often taken up now with formal activities rather than free, exploratory, outdoor play. So now is the time to take up the initiative set many years ago and take your children out on local rambles. Give them the opportunity to explore and discover the secrets of their local area.

Other, more recent work with young children shows that children still take delight in exploring outdoor environments when allowed to and that they notice the minutiae of their surroundings (Owens 2008) as well as, what might be referenced by adults as, the mundane (Ross 2007). Where children have some degree of autonomy as shown in research by Ross (2007) into children's walked journeys to school in Scotland, they readily exhibit spontaneous imaginative play and emotional engagement with their environment.

ACTIVITY BOX **NAME THAT PLACE**

A wonderful activity for children to engage with is to name their own local area, be it the school grounds or their local surroundings. As a teacher you could structure this naming game in a number of ways: purely to see the values and interpretations the children have of such places, or to link to a topic such as a history topic of the United States of America. Could the children name their local area in the style of indigenous Indian groups? So the headteacher's office could be renamed as 'The place of the roaring bear', for example.

Can children research the history of local place names, from street names to the names of local woods and parts of the town?

Children, then, explore a place by doing and have a sense of agency that is determined by childhood's own parameters and their lived-in spatial experiences rather than being informed by watered down versions of adulthood (Matthews and Limb 1999). Fieldwork enquiries can both promote and tap into children's own places and their ways of knowing them but there is a need to balance these more personalised ways of knowing with factual ways of 'knowing' a locality.

CORE KNOWLEDGE AND SENSE OF PLACE

In the last subject report for geography before the advent of Curriculum 2014, Ofsted (2011) advised that fieldwork, core knowledge and a sense of place were all key areas requiring improvement. Arguably, not only are core knowledge and a sense of place aspects of successful fieldwork, they are also connected on a continuum that represents ways of knowing about place (see Figure 4.2).

Places have attributes that can be learnt as facts: they have a location, an accompanying typology such as landscape and climate, and a classification e.g. capital, town, village, etc. However, it should be stressed that in the real world, as noted earlier, facts can be 'messy'. Where does a town begin or end and who says? Is it a political or a geographic boundary or both? Yet there are some things we can say confidently about places that have both a generally recognised truth and an enduring quality e.g. London is the capital of the UK, Africa is a continent, town x has a cinema and a shopping centre and a pedestrianised High Street with commonly agreed names and locations. All are factual statements and whilst they may not necessarily all be true in a thousand years' time or even a hundred, they have a sense of longevity: they are static facts and as such can be learnt and memorised and retold. But this kind of information alone is not geography or fieldwork. It is but a beginning of knowing the complexity of 'place'.

The term 'sense of place' is one that is overused and difficult to pin down but it can be variously regarded as something in our heads, or as a property of landscapes (Relph 2015): it certainly implies less certain and different ways of knowing and perceiving. Places are not static entities but dynamic, multi-faceted entities continually evolving and responding to the interactions that shape them and as Scoffham (2010) noted, emotional and cognitive experiences work together to deepen learning.

Although many aspects of a place can be determined from within a classroom using a range of modern media, maps and other second-hand sources, real world immersive experiences, with personal as well as quantifiable factual data, best contextualises them. But we need to keep in mind that balance of core factual knowledge and the more esoteric

Core knowledge	Sense of place
Static and factual ways of knowing *e.g. St Pancras International Station is located on Euston Road, London N1C 4QP. London is the capital city of England and the UK.*	Perceptual and interpretative connotations of place *e.g. St Pancras is exciting and busy. When I arrive back in St Pancras I feel happy that I am on my way home.*

▨ **Figure 4.2** Balancing core knowledge and a sense of place

and personalised impressions that combine to create both knowledge of and a sense of place.

EMPATHIC GEOGRAPHIES

When we explore a place at first hand we can therefore make sure that as well as enabling a framework of core, factual knowledge, we bring to bear personal impressions too and ways of seeing through rich descriptions, views and interpretations that often rely on sensory and affective methodologies. But we need to recognise the 'other' perspectives too as herein rests the hearts of those intersections or 'knots' of place spoken of by Ingold (2011).

Different individuals and groups of users might view a place in very different terms and have conflicting ideas about how it ought to be used or developed. Children can learn to consider different points of view from a very young age; even reception-age children can, with guidance, talk about their ideas for developing their playground (and give simple reasons why), listen to others and choose actions that take account of all views (Owens 2005).

'Empathic geographies' (Lambert and Owens 2013) describes a process of trying to identify with and feel other points of view when thinking about options and decision-making that affects places and environments. It is a skill to be developed as it involves both emotional engagement and detached rationality but is valuable as children learn that the best decisions must first take account of a range of views. It is only by recognising, analysing and ultimately attempting to understand the myriad responses to a place and the different values and meanings afforded it by different user groups that critical knowing and decision-making can take place. Table 4.1 brings these different kinds of knowing together with suggestions for teaching and learning opportunities and Table 4.2 suggests possible fieldwork activities in more depth.

CRITICAL THINKING

Critical thinking is the twin companion of creativity and gives purpose by focusing in on a range of possibilities (Owens 2017). Without critical thinking, creative endeavours might become woolly, lacking purpose and rigour. In fieldwork, critical thinking doesn't necessarily mean always having to take radical action but it does mean applying gathered knowledge to an outcome that can be valued and which serves a purpose. It requires participative engagement, as opposed to 'tokenism', in which children's views and ideas are truly valued.

FIELDWORK INTO PRACTICE

Risk assessment

Involve children in risk assessment and find out what they know about the area they are going to visit beforehand as well. This is part of good practice for fieldwork (Ofsted 2008) and encourages children to have a greater regard for their own safety when navigating environments. Obviously pupils cannot visit the actual fieldwork site to do a risk assessment (as teachers are obliged to do) but the outside can be brought into the classroom. A risk assessment carried out with pupils can also provide a great context for e.g. geography and English activities.

Table 4.1 Bringing different kinds of knowledge together in fieldwork

Conceptual knowledge	Core knowledge Factual information	Personal knowledge Perceptions and feelings	Empathic knowledge Others' perspectives
Space Key questions	Where is this place?	Where do I think this place is?	What do others think?
T & L opportunities	Use paper and digital maps, globes and atlases to give precise location. Include e.g. postcode, grid references. Identify where you are in the field using GIS and maps.	Could use as a starting assessment to develop children's knowledge about location and ways to do this. Children create their own maps to tell stories of where places are.	Provoke discussion and agree best factual ways to represent a location. Draw and compare made maps.
Scale Key questions	How does this place connect to other places? (Nested hierarchies)	What does 'local' mean? What other places do I know connected to this place?	What connections do others have within and outside of this place?
T & L opportunities	In class, use maps at different scales to e.g. find street names, places and points of interest within a town. Look at the wider picture of how a place is located within other places e.g. county, region, country, etc.	Ask children what places 'within' their locality they know e.g. their own house, the local shops, places they play, and how to get there. Identify wider connections e.g. shopping at nearby towns, visiting relatives, etc.	Children share knowledge. Create a class map of places they know in the locality and those they are linked to in the wider locality.
Place Key questions	What is this place like?	What do I think this place is like? How do I feel about it? What do I do here? What's it got to do with me?	How do others view/see/ feel about this place and why? What other personal and cultural connotations are there?
T & L opportunities	Identify, name, map features using first-hand experience and reliable data sources. Record quantifiable data such as weather, traffic, number of shops, time of day and date, etc.	Use multi-sensory techniques, drawings and photographs to gather ideas about places children notice or are interested in and ask them to give their own descriptions of place. Map these.	Compare views about a place and how these varied. Use views within a class or give questionnaires to others. Look at secondary sources such as newspapers, etc.

Investigate how, where, why and when human and physical geography interacts to create, sustain and change the world around us. Ask how do we fit in? What can we do?

ACTIVITY BOX

■ **Table 4.2** Location detectives

Core knowledge

Map it! Where is this place? Can you give an absolute location? Grid reference? Postcode? Address? GIS reference point?
What key features does this place have at different scales e.g. street, block, city and county level? Use maps at different scales e.g. 1:5000, 1:10000, 1:25000 and 1:50000.

In words: gather place names, street names, signs, shop names, etc. and create word clouds using wordle.net or tagxedo.com. Find place names that give evidence of connections with e.g. former industries, links with the wider world, etc.

In pictures: photograph, film, accurately sketch features and label. Collect views looking in different directions NSEW and clearly label. Collect images at the same place at different times of day or select a route or cross-section and take images at regular intervals. Use wax rubbings to collect textures of building materials.

In numbers: create an infographic/poster of data in numbers. Use a mix of different data representation and see how accurately you can describe a place just in numbers. Count different features, people, measure temperatures and other weather data, traffic, types of activities being carried out, etc.

Personal knowledge

Sound maps: stand still, listen very carefully and try to identify different sounds and the direction they are coming from. Use lines of different length from a centre point to describe distance and direction of the sounds you hear.
Code different sounds, e.g. natural and man-made. Explain what they are and where they are from.

Senses around me: tune in quietly to your surroundings and using your senses, focus on what you can see, smell, hear and feel around you. Write a haiku poem – it is only 3 lines long. The first line has 5 syllables, the second line has 7 syllables and the third line has 5 syllables. OR – just choose five words which you feel best describe the place you are in.

Feel it! How does this place make you feel? Safe? Scary? Relaxed? What emotions will you select? Map your feelings about a place along a route or in a defined area or at one or two identified points.
Use heart-shaped Tagxedo word clouds to summarise reasons why you like a place.

Score it! Devise a set of criteria to evaluate a place using a scaled score for attributes. Or, just evaluate using 'smiley', 'not sure' and 'sad faces' with young children.
Which areas would you most want to change and why/how?

Empathic knowledge

Another view: visit a place in role, e.g. pretend you are looking through the eyes of a toddler, a senior citizen or a disabled person and imagine how they would feel about that place and what they could do there. You could use some cardboard 'empathy' glasses to help get into role!

Community quotes: canvass the local community about their views using pupil-written questionnaires. Invite parents and locals in to view an exhibition of collated views.
Or just gather quick responses from people out and about and record using digital recorders or sticky notes. Link to map.

An ideal spot: imagine you are one of the living non-humans in this place e.g. an animal or a plant, and evaluate the positives and negatives of your location. How ideal is it and why? What do you think would make it better for that living thing and how might it change?

Whose place? How many different users can you see in this place? What are people doing and can you tell what their purpose is? Are some of these users coming into conflict? E.g. drivers and pedestrians?

ACTIVITY BOX **IDENTIFYING HAZARDS**

In class you can use digital imagery to show aerial views of places to be visited and ask pupils to identify and name any features that they can see. Challenge the children to compare and match features using ground views from photographic images, possibly from your own risk assessment visit, and either maps or aerial photographs. Google Earth and Google Maps on the IWB are very good for this. The children can be asked to identify risks from the images and then solutions to stay safe and then when you get to the location see if the children can recognise aspects from the classwork and maps. You could show a number of images showing some key risks and allow time to discuss and note how they could minimise the risks, working in pairs. Finally, an extended writing session can result where pupils use a given writing frame to identify a risk, an action and who is responsible – the latter section is especially important as pupils often think that all actions to mitigate risk lie with other people rather than themselves.

Children take their own responsibilities in this area very seriously and apart from the obvious learning benefits of this kind of preparation, when children take their own risk assessments with them on a trip, it contributes to positive patterns of behaviour.

ACTIVITY BOX **TOP TIPS**

▒ Use photographs at ground level which show a different perspective (e.g. looking East) to an aerial view (e.g. looking North) to challenge thinking about aerial and ground views.

▒ Mark a feature seen from above and again in a ground view to help pupils match aerial to ground perspectives.

▒ A writing frame can be simpler or more complicated – young children can draw pictures and talk about what is happening and who is responsible for their safety.

▒ Let pupils take their risk assessments with them on a trip and ask them to help 'brief' helpers about safety before a trip.

ACTIVITY BOX **OTHERS' VIEWS**

Seeking the views and opinions of others through what has been described as 'empathic geographies' is a powerful dimension of fieldwork. How does this work in practice?

Interviews

Visit carefully selected people in the neighbourhood who do different jobs e.g. holiday park owners, hoteliers, cafe owners, shopkeepers and farmers. Local businesses are often very supportive and keen to make contact with local schools. Arrange times to meet them and arrange who will ask questions beforehand by allocating a group of children to each interviewee.

In class beforehand, give each group of children a short profile of the person they are to interview to help them think of relevant and useful questions linked to their enquiry and help them select what they think will be the best questions from those suggested. You could rehearse asking the questions too to give children confidence. Decide how you will record answers and what you will do with them.

A very positive outcome from meeting people out in the community is that it is mutually beneficial to children and interviewees to learn a little about each other at first hand and challenge any stereotypical assumptions each has about the other. Interactive fieldwork actively tackles problems of social cohesion, helping to build relationships with the local community.

Questionnaires and surveys

Working in closer proximity to the school you could target the immediate area with questionnaires devised by pupils, delivering them by foot to people's homes and / or using email or web site surveys. Spend time in class thinking about the nature of an enquiry and how you will map people's views about the locality and if you can make any recommendations for changes.

When data has been gathered, decide how you will analyse it and who you will share the results with to make it meaningful. From class assemblies to letters to the local paper and the local MP or council, pupils can be proactive in communicating their findings. You could also invite locals into school for an exhibition and talk about local issues.

All of this work offers excellent opportunities for work across the curriculum as well as satisfying specific geographical objectives.

ACTIVITY BOX **TOP TIPS**

- When working out in the wider community think about how long you will be out and practical aspects such as e.g. shelter if the weather is bad, somewhere to eat lunch if out all day and of course toilets. Sometimes these practical aspects and the timetabling and selection of people to visit in the locality can intersect advantageously.
- Build in opportunities for children to review their fieldwork by thinking about what they have learnt and what they might improve next time (see Figure 4.3).
- Keep a fact file of useful contacts and places to visit as well as all risk assessments.
- Invite interviewees into school to see the results of an enquiry and form lasting relationships where possible to deepen learning over time.
- Always try and involve the local press to give activities greater value.

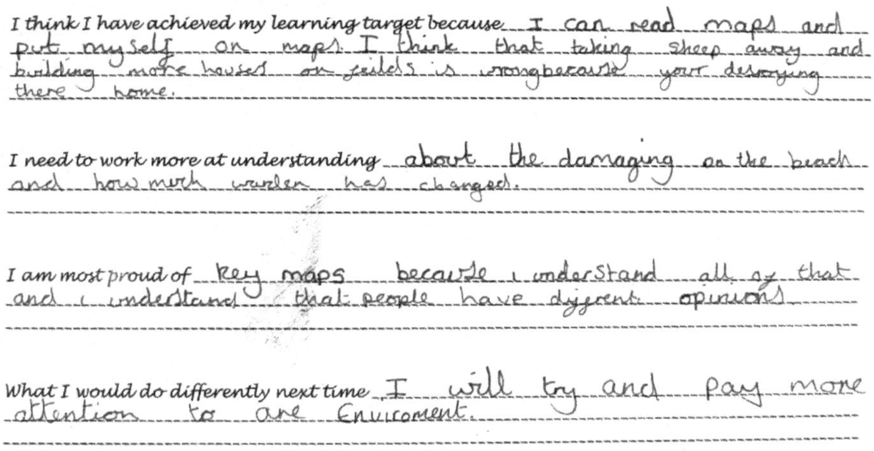

> I think I have achieved my learning target because I can read maps and put myself on maps. I think that taking sheep away and building more houses on fields is wrong because your destroying there home.
>
> I need to work more at understanding about the damaging on the beach and how much warden has changed.
>
> I am most proud of key maps because i understand all of that and i understand that people have different opinions
>
> What I would do differently next time I will try and pay more attention to are Enviroment.

Figure 4.3 Pupil assessment of the Neighbourhood Project

VALUING PLACES

When we spend some time in a place and look at it deeply we encourage bonding and stewardship. When outdoor experiences are driven by children's own curiosity they become even more powerful and create significant memories. How can we engage with local places in meaningful ways?

Habitats

Investigating the health of local habitats whether in the school grounds or further afield and taking actions to improve provision can be both engaging and worthwhile for children. For example bird boxes and feeding stations can be set up reasonably easily. Set up enquiries to find out which animals and plants live locally and which are in decline. Map findings and decide which actions might be taken.

Owls are in decline in many places due to habitat loss. Designing owl boxes for different species of owls and deciding where to site them can be rewarding if your school offers suitable sites or you have access to a nearby area that does. You can research owls or other animals in class as well as visiting areas where they might be found to see them at first-hand or to see the kinds of habitats that support them.

Through habitat studies, children can learn a good deal about the complex relationships between humans, other living things and the environment and also realise that they can make a difference through improving or sustaining environments. Realising that we share spaces with other living things not only improves core knowledge but helps develop values and significant memories: all of which help children develop affective bonds with places. Investigating habitats also provides many opportunities to link geography, science, literacy and maths.

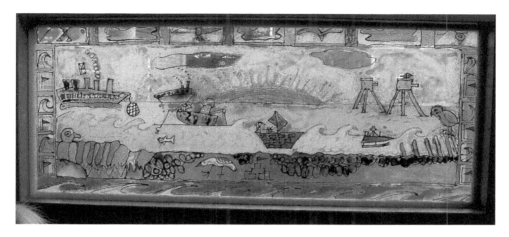

■ **Figure 4.4** A stained glass window designed and created by children

Stained glass windows

Develop a whole school approach to the local area by allocating a specific area and / or aspect of a locality to each year group and carry out a sustained fieldwork enquiry. For example, different locality aspects might include a local street, a park, a local place of worship etc. As part of the enquiry, get children to draw annotated sketches of features and encourage deep observation and discussion about those features that give places a sense of identity and character.

Back in school, create composite pictures of each aspect of area studied using features drawn by children and trace these onto Perspex, outlining with glass paint liners. Children can then collaborate to fill in the features with water-based glass paints. Finally, secure the Perspex panels in place in front of existing windows as long-lasting reminders and talking points. This work could be linked to the storybook *Window* by Jeanne Baker (2002) and to views that correspond with places seen through classroom windows; or they could even be the same places viewed at different seasons; or of the same place before and after a transformation of some kind.

Community maps

Allocate a kilometre square grid of the local area to each class and ask them to create their own map of this area using any style they wish and any media from textiles to collage to paint, and with their own meanings added. Use fieldwork to inform these maps. Put the squares back together to create a large school display highlighting different interpretations. Ensure areas readily accessible from school are given to classes with younger children. Or get each class to study and map the school grounds using meanings from pupils as well as some factual evidence and compare the maps drawn across the school.

THE WAY AHEAD

Many outside agencies such as Groundwork, local heritage centres and nature reserves, local landowners and farmers and community artists will often be willing to contribute to the work of your school and it is worth arranging for the children to contact them to maximise support and possibly access further funding. And of course parents often possess many skills and talents that schools do not harness often enough.

Getting involved

These examples show how children can help direct fieldwork through their own questions and interest; work with the local community to develop understanding about different community roles and issues and learn to see value in and develop attachments to local places. They are all creative and purposeful activities and require core knowledge and a sense of place as well as regard for the core concepts also underpinning rigorous fieldwork. Ultimately though, as places have multi-users with many perspectives, children need to think about some of the big umbrella questions that drive fieldwork enquiry such as whose place is this? Who decides? What's it got to do with me? And why should I care?

■ **Figure 4.5** Children interviewing a farmer on a visit

REFERENCES

Association of Science Education (ASE) (2011) *Outdoor Science: A Co-ordinated Approach to High-quality Teaching and Learning in Fieldwork for Science Education. A Report by the Association for Science Education Outdoor Science Working Group.* London: FSC and King's College.

Baker, J. (2002) *Window.* London: Walker Books.

Catling, S., Greenwood, R., Martin, F. and Owens, P. (2010) Formative experiences of primary geography educators. *International Research in Geographical and Environmental Education* 19(4): 341–350.

DfE (2014) *The National Curriculum in England Framework for Key Stages 1 to 4.* Available at: www.gov.uk/government/publications/national-curriculum-in-england-framework-for-key-stages-1-to-4 (accessed February 2016).

Foreman, M. (1993) *Dinosaurs and All That Rubbish.* London: Puffin Books.

GA (2009) *A Different View: A Manifesto from the Geographical Association.* Sheffield: Geographical Association. Available at: www.geography.org.uk/resources/adifferentview/#top (accessed 21 November 2016).

Gibson, J.J. (1979) *The Ecological Approach to Visual Perception.* Boston: Houghton Mifflin.

Hart, R. (1978) *Children's Experience of Place: A Developmental Study.* New York: Irvington Publishers (distributed by Halstead/Wiley Press). Available at: http://cergnyc.org/files/2013/12/Hart_Childrens-Experience-of-Place.pdf (accessed January 2016).

Hart, R. (2015) *It's All Academic: Kids' Geography.* Radio interview Friday 13 February 2015 6:50PM. Available at: www.abc.net.au/radionational/programs/drive/it27s-all-academic3a-kids27-geography/6093778 (accessed February 2016).

Hicks, D. (2014) *Educating for Hope in Troubled Times.* London: Institute of Education Press.

Ingold, T. (2011) *Being Alive: Essays on Movement, Knowledge and Description.* Oxon: Routledge.

Lambert, D. and Owens, P. (2013) in Jones, R. and Wyse, D. (eds) *Creativity in the Primary Curriculum.* Abingdon: David Fulton.

Lambert, D. and Reiss, M.J. (2014) *The Place of Fieldwork in Geography and Science Qualifications.* London: Institute of Education, University of London.

Louv, R. (2013) *Last Child in the Woods: Saving our Children from Nature-Deficit Disorder.* London: Atlantic Books.

Matthews, H. and Limb, M. (1999) Defining an agenda for the geography of children: review and prospect. *Progress in Human Geography* 23(1): 61–90.

Merriman, P., Jones, M., Olsson, G., Sheppard, E., Thrift, N. and Tuan, Y.F. (2012) Space and spatiality in theory. *Dialogues in Human Geography* 2(1): 3–22.

Ofsted (2008) *Geography – Changing Practice. Making Fieldwork a Focus.* London: HMSO.

Ofsted (2011) *Geography – Learning to Make a World of Difference.* London: HMSO.

Owens, P. (2005) Children's environmental values in the early school years. *International Research in Geographical and Environmental Education* 14(4): 323–329.

Owens, P. (2008) Take a walk on the child side. *Primary Geography* 67. Sheffield, Geographical Association, pp. 25–28.

Owens, P. (2017) Geography and sustainability. In Scoffham, S. (ed.) *Teaching Geography Creatively*, 2e. London: Routledge, pp.177–192.

Pickering, S. (2017) Keeping Geography messy. In Scoffham, S. (ed.) *Teaching Geography Creatively*, 2e. London: Routledge, pp.198–204.

Pretty, J., Angus, C., Bain, M., Barton, J., Gladwell, V., Hine, R., Pilgrim, S., Sandercock, S. and Sellens, M. (2009) *Nature, Childhood, Health and Life Pathways.* Interdisciplinary Centre for Environment and Society Occasional Paper 2009–02. University of Essex.

Relph, E. (2015) *Sense of Place: An Overview.* Available at: www.placeness.com/sense-of-place-an-overview (accessed February 2016).

Rickinson, M., Hunt, A., Rogers, J. and Dillon, J. 2012. *School Leader and Teacher Insights into Learning Outside the Classroom in Natural Environments.* Natural England Commissioned Reports, Number 097.

Ross, N.J. (2007) 'My journey to school . . .': foregrounding the meaning of school journeys and children's engagements and interactions in their everyday localities. *Children's Geographies* 5(4): 373–391.

Scoffham, S. (2010) Young geographers. In Scoffham, S. (ed.) *Primary Geography Handbook.* Sheffield: Geographical Association, pp. 15–23.

Stables, A. (1998) Proximity and distance: moral education and mass communication. *Journal of Philosophy of Education*, 32: 399–407.

Tuan, Yi-Fu (1977) *Space and Place: The Perspective of Experience.* Minneapolis: University of Minnesota Press.

UN (2015) *Sustainable Development Goals: 17 Goals to Transform Our World.* Available at: www.un.org/sustainabledevelopment (accessed February 2016).

UNESCO (2014) *Position Paper on Education Post-2015 ED-14/EFA/POST-2015/1* Available at: http://unesdoc.unesco.org/images/0022/002273/227336E.pdf (accessed February 2016).

STORYING THE OUTDOORS

Sharon Witt

INTRODUCTION

Stories can connect people and places and so offer creative possibilities to stimulate children's engagement with the outdoors. This chapter explores the potential of a particular kind of narrative approach that seeks to animate children's real world encounters. 'Storywork' outdoors aims to foster relationships and support children's developing knowledge and understanding of the world around them. Principles of practice for a place responsive storied approach will be shared where children and teachers are engaged actively, imaginatively and attentively in environmental explorations. This places the outdoors at the centre of the creative learning process.

STORY AS AN INVITATION

Story is at the heart of being human. People are essentially storytellers and narration is one of the first language skills all children develop; narrative seems to be universal across cultures and times. 'By providing children with learning experiences constructed around story we are giving them opportunities to learn, within a framework that coincides with the way they structure thought' (Daniel 2012, p.11). Stories are linked to ancient ways of knowing and are one of the fundamental ways in which humans come to understand the world. Storying the outdoors invites teachers and children to engage, connect and build relationships with places out of doors. As Wattchow and Brown (2011, p.180) suggest, outdoor places are 'rich in significance and meaning' and a 'powerful pedagogic phenomenon'. Stories created outdoors can provide children with 'fuel for imagination and inspiration' (MacLellan, 2007, p.165). Creative teachers also recognise the story potential rooted in local landscapes for developing children's knowledge and sense of place, creative and reflective thinking, enquiry and problem solving skills and descriptive language.

When working outdoors children are creating their own personal narrative of adventure and exploration encountering the new, the unfamiliar and the unexpected. They create new stories of place based on their unique ways of seeing and being in that place with others. Stories in places often have an educative purpose as they are tied up with sense of self, sense of belonging and a sense of the community in which the children are working (Basso, 1996). Knowledge of places is therefore closely linked to knowledge of the self, to grasping one's own position in the larger scheme of things, including one's own community, and to securing a confident sense of who one is as a person. Teachers can support children's story making by offering a range of playful, immersive, sensory stimuli to provoke children's attention to the detail of environments and imbue outdoor spaces with personal meaning. As children's relationships with a setting develop and change through storied experiences, they begin to develop a deeper sense of place and place attachment. With space and time children can become attached to these places and make meaning of these experiences through sharing and celebrating their stories of outdoor places. 'Stories are the most immediate and personal medium of conveying experience and information' (Daniel 2012, p.11) and provide teacher and child with the opportunity to share perspectives on events and ideas.

With contemporary concerns regarding disconnection with the outdoors, story provides an opportunity for teachers and children to forge relationships with the world. Within a curriculum that is focused on performativity and accountability an emphasis on story could be seen by some as a 'frivolous or fanciful endeavour' yet 'it is a serious attempt to connect and make sense of where we are and who we are' (Wattchow and Brown, 2011, p.180). In this way there are links to the social, moral, spiritual, cultural (SMSC) dimension within schools. Stories offer teachers a way to (re)animate the outdoors for children and provide opportunities for lively spirited enquiry. A narrative approach offers new perspectives for children to see the world as exciting, joyful and offering a sense of wonder. Stories open up opportunities for the sites of outdoor learning to become spaces of acquaintance where children come to know and connect with local environments. This suggests the relationships between children, their teacher and the elements of place are important. The ecologist Gregory Bateson (1979) believed that stories were the language of this relationship between humans and the living world.

Outdoor places where stories are waiting to be told

Outdoor stories may be told about the environment, in the environment and through the environment. Local myths, legends and folk tales have long shared the rich social, cultural and historical traditions of places. Through oral storytelling traditions, ancient cultures have passed on historical, social and cultural messages to younger generations. The narratives that are embedded in a culture's landscapes and memory can be viewed both as stories that connect us and stories that make us different (Cameron, 2004). This chapter aims to recognise that individuals possess multiple and unique stories of outdoor places. It plans to focus on a particular idea of storying the outdoors with children through a notion of place responsiveness.

Place responsiveness emphasises the possibilities that unfold when children are immersed in the outdoors. Personal stories emerge from direct observation and embodied encounters. It is about children spending time outdoors, sharing their personal geographies, giving names to favourite places, to tell and retell stories of adventures and allow them to celebrate the outdoor encounters that 'touch their soul' (Raffan, 1993, p.45). A place responsive approach is underpinned by the belief that stories reside in places and people and story plays a significant role in outdoor experiences (Wattchow and Brown, 2011). This approach makes outdoor places come alive – they become stories of placefulness. It encourages a relational way of knowing and acknowledges the human, the non-human and the more than human elements that exist within the environment. It recognises that 'landscape is loud with dialogues, with storylines that connect a place and its dwellers' (Spirn, 1998, p.17) and requires children and teachers to be carefully attentive to the world through the use of their senses and being open to exchanging messages between humans and the world. It acknowledges an imaginative dimension to learning. As Waters (2011, p.244) writes, 'children are remarkably perceptive to stories and narratives that draw them into a world of make believe; it's as if they are naturally tuned to perceive the world as playful and that play itself is a way of being'.

This storied approach to environmental encounters requires children to read the landscape and to notice and attend to potential story stimuli that can lead to practical activity in outdoor places. This approach draws on Gibson's theory of affordances (1979) and acknowledges that children's outdoor explorations are constantly informed by the affordances of place. Affordance can be understood as what a place allows or invites children to do. For example, a bank of soft green moss may encourage children to sit, a hill may invite children to roll down it and a tree with low branches may encourage a child to climb into its branches. This entangled and highly personal relationship between individuals and their environments can lead to multiple and unique stories of place.

Stories created through a place responsive approach need to include both felt, embodied encounters with a place and an engagement with knowing the place through various cultural knowledge systems, such as ecology, geography, history. For example, a place responsive visit undertaken by children to Selborne Field Studies Centre in the grounds of the home of the curate and naturalist Gilbert White might involve a journey around the historic and cultural site. The teacher may sometimes encourage the children to explore independently in 'a field of free action' and at other times may structure their experience to encourage engagement through 'promoted action' offering activities that will provoke sensory awareness and curiosity (Waters, 2011, p.246). Teachers and children look, listen, touch and immerse themselves in the site to see characters, plots and themes emerge in the moment (Waters, 2014). The Selborne outdoor experiences may include walks in the beech woodland, exploration of the village and Gilbert White's house, where there are also connections to stories of polar expeditions and visits to the garden. As they journey it is hoped that the children notice the woodland welcome that resides in the place (see Figure 5.1). They might paddle in the stream as they undertake a river study, they may make 'leaf angels' immersing themselves in the leaves of that place, they may engage in making homes for the hidden folk of the wood and they may mould story characters from clay found on the site. The features within this Hampshire landscape will capture the children and teachers' attention and act as way markers for stories.

Growing your own place responsive stories

A storied approach to outdoor pedagogy places the location and setting of the story at the heart of an outdoor environmental experience. It offers new perspectives for children to see the world as exciting, joyful and offering a sense of wonder. As Van Matre (1990, p.201) writes: 'You always go adventuring expecting that something special will happen. You expect to discover new things. It is a delicious sense of setting out just knowing that you are going to find something new that propels you.' Four core aspects of storying the outdoors are exploration; engagement; connection; and response (see Table 5.1). These elements are non-hierarchical and not discrete aspects of practice. They are not to be delivered in a linear way but should be allowed to overlap and interlink to assemble place-based stories. It is helpful to let enquiry questions drive children's discoveries and curiosity. Inspired by Wattchow and Brown (2011) these questions could include:

■   What stories can we find in this place?
■   What is in this place?
■   What does this place invite us to do?
■   Who (human and non-human) lives here?
■   Who relies upon this place?
■   How can we be attentive to this place?
■   What does this place know?
■   How does this place share its wisdom?
■   Where can this place take us?

In Table 5.1 I offer some suggestions to support teachers as they develop a storied approach to outdoor encounters. These approaches can support teachers' place responsive curriculum making, but as teachers plan they will need to tailor these ideas to the specific context of each individual site; different places will suggest unique responses. The planning of this kind of storied experience should not be completed in isolation from the setting –

■ **Table 5.1** 'Storying Place' processes

		Possible activities
EXPLORING Beginning to actively investigate the environment	Introducing the outdoors setting as a stimulus to children's stories Getting to know the outdoors	Sensing – touching, smelling, hearing, seeing, tasting, emotions Observing and noticing Exploration/discovery Raising questions Curiosity
ENGAGING Active participation and involvement in the world	Developing acquaintance with places	Participating in the outdoors Create a context for engagement with the outdoors: adventure, search, quest, hunt, mystery, event, mission . . . Playing, imagining, enquiry
CONNECTING Creating place attachments	Tuning in to the outdoors Reciprocal relationship developing between outdoors and children	Attention to the environment Looking for: clues, signs, secrets of place, symbols, alternative perspectives, different views, artefacts Reflecting
RESPONDING Recording relationships and participation in the outdoor world	Celebrate outdoor experiences Making meaning and memories	Stories shared through: telling, writing, book creation, dancing, parading, photographs, drawing, poetry, sculpture, song, place making e.g. den building

Figure 5.1
A woodland welcome from the
trees in the Selborne Hangers

teachers should visit the location for their encounters as inspiration comes from the place and the people you meet there.

It takes time to tell the full story of a place

Opportunities to take children outdoors are precious and time is limited within today's primary curriculum. Schools have a limited number of hours in which they have to meet the expectations of a broad and balanced curriculum. Creative teachers recognise the value of spending time in the natural world with their children and recognise that supporting children's developing connection to the outdoors cannot be hurried; it takes time. When teachers adopt a slow pedagogical approach to storying the outdoors their children are invited 'to pause or dwell in spaces for more than a fleeting moment' (Payne and Wattchow, 2009, p.16). This slow pedagogy does not imply a lethargic or sluggish attitude to outdoor exploration. In fact by embracing a deliberate and patient approach to environmental encounters place acquaintance can be fostered through first hand, sensorial experience of the world. As Richard Louv (2005, p.117) reminds us, 'it takes time – loose, unstructured dreamtime – to experience nature in a meaningful way'. This can nurture a deeper and more profound understanding of the world. Given time, opportunities to story the outdoors can support the children to establish an active relationship with the world, transforming abstract spaces into meaningful places. One strategy teachers can use to aid the 'slowing down' of outdoor exploration is the use of thinking routines (Project Zero, 2015). These routines can guide children's thinking, encouraging active processing of their surroundings. They provide a simple frame or series of steps for children to follow in order to spark curiosity fostering local place enquiries and observation with purpose. In searching for

BOX 5.1 I SEE, I THINK, I WONDER . . .

'I see . . . a floating leaf.
I think . . . magic is holding it up.
I wonder . . . How is it spinning? How long has it been there? Who is making the magic?'
'I see . . . a tree.
I think . . . it has poisonous berries.
I wonder . . . how many are on the tree? How long has it been there?'

(Thackrah, 2017)

stories of wonder in the school grounds one teacher used the visible thinking routine: **I see, I think, I wonder** . . . with a group of 8 and 9 year olds and recorded the children's thoughts and questions in a wonder book (see Box 5.1).

Another frame that teachers have used successfully to invite children to move beyond the superficial is: **Pause, Peer and Ponder** (Love, Seymour and Witt, 2015). This series of words hints at a sequence of actions that engages children in a slow enquiry process encouraging them to create carefully observed stories of place and reflect on how they are making sense of the world. This slow pedagogy values possibilities, respects multiple perspectives and aims for 'resilience, harmony and the preservation of patterns that connect' (Orr, 2002, p.39). Both of these thinking routines are flexible and can be used to engage children within different outdoor settings. They nurture an unhurried process of exploration and story creation. A reciprocal relationship between the children and the outdoors can be fostered with opportunities to be still, to sit and be present and mindful in nature. These quiet moments can often help children to attend to outdoor places.

Tales of looking closely

Creative teachers can offer techniques of attention that can engage children with the outdoors and help them to animate the landscape. One technique that has been used successfully is the use of miniature figures in outdoor environments. This work has been inspired by the book *Little People in the City: The Street Art of Slinkachu* (Slinkachu, 2008). Children respond well to being given some freedom to create stories as suggested by the landscapes they inhabit. Miniaturisation is a powerful pedagogic technique that encourages the children to see a place in a particular way. It can encourage children to look at the detail of outdoor places from many different angles and perspectives to unlock its true value and potential (Witt and Clarke, 2014). Younger children may use Lego or Duplo characters or even woodland creatures e.g. Sylvanian families. Older children are fascinated by railway figures that are very small in scale, but realistic. The children are keen to look, to hold and to name their 'little people'. The children can be encouraged to 'place' them in the landscape and can record their miniature tales or storied journeys around different sites using photographs, videos and book creator apps. The combination of figures and landscape can spark creative responses that are innovative, ingenious, playful and humorous. On an explorative journey around Hopetoun House, a stately home in Queensferry, Edinburgh, children used miniature figures in different ways to tell the stories of the place. These included:

■ Drawing attention to sites that were significant to them e.g. the pet cemetery, the view across to the Forth Road Bridge, an ancient cannon. These were sites of curiosity and the figures helped to highlight their value to the children.

■ Working collaboratively and making decisions with others to create stories, scenarios and raps. The children became a community of place storytellers.

■ Using them to highlight issues of the site e.g. where the rubbish bins were located.

■ Creating story trails which were recorded with the characters showing the route to be followed. This could be drawn into a story map.

■ Identifying risks. One child found a particularly muddy path which he wanted to advise people about and so used his miniature figure to warn others (see Figure 5.2).

■ Enhancing children's appreciation of the place. Photographs of figures were taken in situ to show the shapes, textures and views of the location.

■ Raising questions – Who lives behind this door? What view is through this very tall window?

The possibilities are endless and limited only by the children's imaginations. Many of the activities above have described placing a figure in the environment but children can also engage in place making for their 'little people'. They enjoy the agency and immediacy that creating small worlds provides. It encourages children to 'look beyond things as they are, and anticipate what might be seen through a new perspective or through another's eyes' (Greene, 1988, p.49). What is the view of the little figure? How might they view the humans? Do the children appear like giants to the little people? This opens opportunities to consider aspects of scale and offers potential to build stories around small worlds using fiction as a stimulus e.g. *The Minpins* by Roald Dahl (1991) or *The Borrowers* by Mary Norton (2011). Teachers could provide children with different scenarios to provoke the children's storying. These may include:

■ build a house to attract more little people to the woods;

■ build a sustainable community;

■ **Figure 5.2**
Miniature figures used to highlight risky areas around the site

■ a place for little people to relax;
■ a place with a view;
■ create scenes and take photographs to tell the story of your little people's community – make sure the photographs of your figures show action, posture and gesture to demonstrate their emotions.

Another technique creative teachers may use to animate the world is through the use of googly eyes is a technique known as 'eyebombing'. This involves attaching googly eyes to artefacts in the environment in a way that brings the location alive. This encourages the children to see the world from a different view and encourages close observation. One group of eight year olds enjoyed travelling around their school grounds looking for potential locations for their 'eyes'. They were invited by their teacher to take an empathetic stance and consider what their googly eyed character might see, feel, know. It was suggested to the children that their character possessed a lot of place wisdom as they were able to watch who used the space around them and what the local issues might be. The children were invited to record their 'place person' in photographs and tell stories of their experiences. If teachers are uneasy about using plastic within the environment an alternative would be to draw eyes on the children's hands to create natural creatures that might inhabit a place (see Figure 5.3).

These playful activities, such as googly eyes and miniature people, can engage children in activities fostering their ability 'to see the extraordinary' and 'from this an ecological imagination emerges' (Judson, 2010, p.4). This ecological imagination encourages children 'to see (and hear, and feel) beyond the visible world' (Fettes, 2005, p.3). Magnifying glasses or mirrors can encourage the children to look closely at their

■ **Figure 5.3**
Animating the world – what might this tree see, hear, feel or notice?

environment. Exploring their school grounds one group of eleven year olds became convinced they could see a face in the tree, and that the tree represented a person! They also used mirrors to look up into the tree canopy. What does this look like? What could the branches represent? The children offered ideas such as 'an exploding blender', 'Einstein's hair' and 'interlocking finger tips' (Witt and Clarke, 2014).

Stories of playfulness and imagination

By opening the children's imaginations to the unforeseen forces of the natural world it may be possible to restore an ecological dimension to children's learning, for Blizard and Schuster (2007, p.175) suggest that 'when a landscape becomes peopled by story, human beings begin to develop a sense of reverence for it'. Stories give humans a sense of place or a sense of homeland. The importance of play as a major activity in a child's relationship with nature is well recognised (Kalvaitis and Monhardt, 2012) and playful interactions offer a powerful stimulus to place storying. Storied playful encounters with places can lead to relationships of respect, care and stewardship of the natural world.

IN THE COMPANY OF TROLLS

Inspired by Pilkington's book *Trolls – Philosophy and Wisdom*, one teacher ventured into the landscape with their class. Pilkington (2011) unsettles traditional views of trolls as 'repugnant and hostile' to humans and shares a view that trolls are 'reticent, serene and highly intelligent beings living in harmony with nature'. This book engages children with traditional characters from Icelandic folklore and encourages the children to travel in places with an open mind. After being introduced to Pilkington's troll wisdom through the words 'Listen to nature long enough and it will communicate with you', the children became attentive and responsive to their surroundings. They spotted potential homes for trolls in the landscape; they began to tell each other troll stories and began to look carefully for signs and symbols that the landscape may be inhabited by other beings. Stories began to emerge from the children as they connected to their surroundings, viewing them in wonder as a place of possibilities. The children began to notice shapes and figures and could see trolls' feet and faces within the woodland they were travelling in (Figure 5.4). Their wonder at the outdoors began to manifest itself in discovery, fantasy and enquiry as they engaged

■ **Figure 5.4**
Children spotted trolls' feet in the landscape

with an imaginative dimension to their learning and began to view the woods differently. In these times of increased accountability this kind of lesson may be viewed by some as superficial and unnecessary, focusing as it does on the aspects of learning which are difficult to measure. However, Trotman (2014) suggests that a curriculum which enables wonder to flourish and makes meaningful connections to the lives of children is now more necessary than ever. It also provides opportunities for writing to emerge from these encounters, whether real or imagined. The awe and wonder of the real world comes alive in the children's imaginings.

In search of dragons

Dragonology (Steer, 2013) or the study of dragons can be worth pursuing to create place responsive stories that engage and excite both children and teachers. One school has used tales of these mythical creatures to guide their explorations of the Welsh landscape around the Brecon Beacons. Their adventure was called the Dragon of Libanus (Witt, 1999). The children's outdoor adventure began on the first night of their residential. A teacher told an adapted story of Vortigern's Castle in the dark, atmospheric ruins of the motte and bailey fortress, Bronllys Castle. The tale told of the failed construction of a castle because two dragons were fighting in the foundations of the building. They were disturbed by the builders and one flew to the light of the mountain and the other to the darkness of the Black Lake. The story relayed a challenge for a set of brave and caring people to bring the two dragons together in peace. The children found a scroll on their second morning that suggested 'the power of the dragon is in the earth, is in the air, is in fire, and is in water'. This challenge hooked the children into their outdoor learning experience and they enjoyed following a set of riddles and clues that guided them on a quest as they climbed Pen-y-fan, walked behind a waterfall at Sgwd yr Eira, visited caves at Porth-yr-Ogof and flew kites on the dragon mounds of the common by the National Park Visitors Centre. This storied approach which required the children to work within a community of creative explorers allowed teachers to add an extra element to the children's experience which they would not get on a family holiday or on a guided fieldtrip. Through storying the location children gained a heightened awareness of landscape. One child spoke of liking 'the pleated hills' whilst another spoke of reaching the top of the mountain as a great achievement. She recalled:

> I noticed as I was climbing out of the corner of my eye everything seemed to be getting smaller and moving away from me and then when you stopped and looked it was like . . . wow ! I felt I had conquered my fears when I got there and it was like . . . wow!

Another child spoke of how the land looked beautiful like a patchwork quilt. There was evidence that the children were beginning to attend to the detail of the Welsh landscape. A highlight of the visit was the building of dragon nests within local woodland intended to lure both the red and white dragons to a place where they might find peace together. The children re-visited the nests later in the week to find chocolate 'dragon eggs' had mysteriously appeared courtesy of some enthusiastic teachers. Following the visit one child stated 'Wales was really magical. I loved the stories and the castle and finding the clues'. Making magical experiences arose from weaving a story to create a special atmosphere and it is hoped that if this approach is properly implemented the 'experience enhances and intensifies the magic of nature' (Van Matre, 1990, p.203). Storying place with trolls, dragons and other mystical creatures can encourage the children to open up to outdoor places and make connections that are unexpected, surprising and beyond the ordinary. They nurture the construction of deep emotional and cultural connections to places as sites of knowing and inspiration. Storied approaches to outdoor encounters can have a profound impact on children. Following the visit one child shared their diary entry that revealed a sense of connection with the unknown and an attachment to place:

> Dragon, I haven't seen you and I know I will never see you. But you will always be there in the earth, air, fire and water. Thank you.

CONCLUSION

Place responsive storying values cognitive, physical, emotional and imaginative dimensions of learning. Creative teachers can empower children to become storytellers of their outdoor place experiences. They can help children to pay greater attention to how particular places invite us to learn and how tales of these experiences within places can be told. This will help children and teachers to make sense of the world around them and see possibilities for actions and responses. Research evidence suggests that when places are brought alive through story they can become 'places of initiation' where borders between the children and non-human elements in the environment become blurred and 'where the earth gets under our nails and a sense of place gets under our skin' (Pyle, 1993, p.3). A storied approach to outdoor places can support teachers to nourish habits such as noticing, listening, touching and feeling that children may need to build a kinship with the outdoor places. It is hoped that this chapter has shared ideas and experiences for a spirited enquiry of outdoor places that 'linger in the heart' (Raffan, 1993, p.39) and help to build deep, respectful, reciprocal relationships that will remain with the children for a life time.

REFERENCES

Basso, K. (1996) Wisdom sits in places. In S. Feld and K. H. Basso (eds) *Senses of place*, Santa Fe, NM: School of American Research Press.

Bateson, G. (1979) *Mind and Nature: A Necessary Unity*, London: Wildwood House.

Blizard, C. R. and Schuster, R. M. (2007) Fostering children's connections to natural places through cultural and natural history storytelling. *Children, Youth and Environments,* 17(4), 171–206.

Cameron, J. I. (2004) S*ome Implications of Malpas' Place and Experience for Place Ethics and Education*. Available at: www.arch.ksu.edu/seamon/cameron_malpas.htm (accessed 11 March 2016).

Dahl, R. (1991) *The Minpins*, London: Jonathan Cape Children's Books.

Daniel, A. K. (2012) *Storytelling Across the Primary Curriculum*, Abingdon: Routledge.

Fettes, M. (2005) Imaginative transformation in teacher education. *Teaching Education,* 16(1), 3–11.

Gibson, J. J. (1979) *The Ecological Approach to Visual Perception*, Boston: Houghton-Mifflin.

Greene, M. (1988) *The Dialectic of Freedom*, New York: Teachers College Press.

Judson, G. (2010) *A New Approach to Ecological Education. Engaging Students' Imaginations in Their World,* New York: Peter Lang.

Kalvaitis, D. and Monhardt, R. M. (2012) The architecture of children's relationships with nature: a phenomenographic investigation seen through drawings and written narratives of elementary students. *Environmental Education Research*, 18(2), 209–227.

Louv, R. (2005) *Last Child in the Woods*, North Carolina: Algonquin Books.

Love, R., Seymour, M. and Witt, S. (2015) *Fostering Geographical Wisdom*, Charney Manor Primary Research Conference, 27 February–1 March.

MacLellan, G. (2007) *Celebrating Nature*, Somerset: Capall Bann Publishing.

Norton, M. (2011) *The Borrowers,* London: Puffin.

Orr, D. (2002) *The Nature of Design. Ecology, Culture and Human Intention*, Oxford: Oxford University Press.

Payne, P. G. and Wattchow, B. (2009) Phenomenological deconstruction, slow pedagogy, and the corporeal turn in wild environmental/outdoor education, *Canadian Journal of Environmental Education*, 14, 15–32.

Pilkington, B. (2011) *Trolls – Philosophy and Wisdom* , Reykjavik: Mál og Menning.

Project Zero (2015) *Visible Thinking,* Harvard Graduate School of Education. Available at: www.pz.harvard.edu/projects/visible-thinking (accessed 5 March 2016).

Pyle, R. (1993) *The Thunder Trees: Lessons from an Urban Wildland,* Boston: Houghton Mifflin.

Raffan, J. (1993) Experience of place: exploring land as teacher, *Journal of Experiential Education*, 16(1), 39–45.

Slinkachu (2008) *Little People in the City: the Street Art of Slinkachu*, London: Boxtree.

Spirn, A. W. (1998) *The Language of Landscape,* London: Yale University Press.

Steer, D. A. (2013) *Dr Ernest Drake's Dragonology*, Dorking: Templar Publishing.

Thackrah, I. (2017) *Our Everyday Wonderland*, Primary Geography.

Trotman, D. (2014) Wow! What if? So what? Education and the imagination of wonder: fascination, possibilities and opportunities missed. In Egan, K., Cant, A. and Judson, G. (eds) *Wonder-Full Education: The Centrality of Wonder in Teaching and Learning across the Curriculum*, Oxon: Routledge.

Van Matre, S. (1990) *Earth Education: A New Beginning*, West Virginia: Institute of Earth Education.

Waters, P. (2011) Trees talk: are you listening? Nature, narrative and children's anthropocentric place-based play. *Children Youth and Environments*, 21(1), 243–252.

Waters, P. (2014) Narrative journey: storying landscapes for children's adventurous outdoor play and experiential learning. *Horizons*, 67(4), 32–35.

Wattchow, B. and Brown, M. (2011) Signposts to a place-responsive pedagogy in outdoor education. In Wattchow, B. and Brown, M. (eds) *A Pedagogy of Place: Outdoor Education for a Changing World*, Melbourne: Monash University Publishing, pp.180–199.

Witt, S. (1999) *The use of residential visits as a vehicle to promote social, moral, spiritual, cultural development,* unpublished dissertation for MA(Ed), University of Southampton.

Witt, S. and Clarke, H. (2014) *Eco-playfulness: storied encounters with nature to re(imagine) new relationships with a meaningful curriculum*. Presentation at Teacher Education for Equity and Sustainability (TEESNet) Seventh Annual Conference 10 July, Liverpool Hope University.

FOREST SCHOOL

Opportunities for creative and spiritual growth

Sara Knight

INTRODUCTION

Since the earliest research observations of Forest School activities were reported (Borradaile, 2006; Hughes, 2007; O'Brien and Murray, 2007) we have been aware of the impact of Forest School on children's sense of wellbeing. What has not been articulated clearly is why that might happen. In this chapter I intend to look at the underpinning principles guiding the delivery of Forest School sessions to see how they link to the 'why'. My contention is that we have an innate need for a spiritual domain which modern life fails to offer many of us, and that Forest School provides space and time for participants to explore both their spirituality and their creativity through nature, connecting with their inner selves through connecting with the outer wilder world. For young children Forest School can represent a return to an evolutionary animistic past that resonates with many children, not as a replacement for whatever formal religions that may be a part of their cultural lives, but as a comforting and safe place for exploring their individual sense of self and their place in the world. And it is these experiences that offer children and adults opportunities for true unregulated creativity that is often missing in more structured spaces.

The Forest School Association in the UK (Forest School Association, 2015), which is a bottom-up association of practitioners and practitioner-trainers, consulted their membership in 2011–12 to draw together six guiding principles governing the delivery of good quality Forest School. These are published on their website, referenced above. Whilst they have no legislative force and there are sessions which badge themselves as 'Forest School' which do not follow these principles, there is a general acceptance that these are what are needed to be followed to achieve the outcomes recorded by the observers cited above. I will step through them, demonstrating how these principles also form a platform for creative and spiritual growth.

PRINCIPLE 1: FOREST SCHOOL IS A LONG-TERM PROCESS OF FREQUENT AND REGULAR SESSIONS IN A WOODLAND OR NATURAL ENVIRONMENT, RATHER THAN A ONE-OFF VISIT. PLANNING, ADAPTATION, OBSERVATIONS AND REVIEWING ARE INTEGRAL ELEMENTS OF FOREST SCHOOL

Forest School practitioners are aiming to establish long-lasting patterns of behaviour and long-lasting positive perceptions of nature in participants. We know that in early childhood neural pathways are developed by repeated exposure to stimuli and by repetitions of actions and events. Thus, regular Forest School sessions with children from the age of three up to the end of the English Key Stage 1, roughly seven years old, are laying the foundations for lives that include outdoor exercise and a love of nature. They are also developing the qualities recorded by researchers: of confidence, good self-esteem, social and emotional resilience and good communication skills.

Where practitioners are working with older children and adults they are aware that changing behaviour takes longer than establishing behaviours during the relevant sensitive periods in a child's normal development. For these reasons Forest School takes place regularly, ideally at least once a week, and over an extended period of time. The precise length will be different for different ages and purposes. What these changes *are* have started to be recorded, as indicated above, but thus far the research has mostly focused on those elements preselected by commissioning groups. These tend to be the things that policy-makers believe will enable participants to succeed educationally, such as language skills and teamworking skills, as for the most part the commissioning agencies have been looking for justifications for expenditure from tightening educational budgets. However, some recent research from the field of ecotherapy is demonstrating that being in the natural world is helping participants to understand better the 'relationship between human wholeness and the integrity of the natural world, leading to a sense of harmony' (Burls, 2007).

This newer strand of research comes from increasing health concerns around obesity and mental health in the developed world. In 2009 Natural England coined the term 'Natural Health Service' (Natural England, 2009), following it up with a *Manifesto for the Natural Environment* in 2010. These health-facing researchers are pointing at a necessary link between humans and nature as articulated by Wilson (1984), who coined the term biophilia to describe that link. Vining, Merrick and Price (2008) found a positive correlation between positive emotions and feeling connected to nature by virtue of the amount of time spent in the natural world. The more unspoilt the nature, the stronger the link.

Also important for this chapter is the thought that the best environmental engagements will take place if the duration of the sessions encompasses all the seasons. I have highlighted before (Knight, 2011: 56) the benefits of the UK climate with its four distinct seasons, a bonus for all living in temperate climates. These changes impact on the wellbeing and innate creativity of participants in two ways. Herbert (2010: 86) speaks of the danger when repetition blocks creativity, but when in nature repeating a session in a wooded space offers experiences of constant change as the seasons progress. This enables the participant to relax by being in a familiar space, developing a sense of place that facilitates a receptive frame of mind and at the same time being stimulated by the observation of changes in that space to be creative. Chawla (2007) writes about 'ecstatic places', those natural places and occasions that enable us to experience a heightened awareness, so that often familiar and loved spaces in one moment can gift us with a special focus – it may be the dew on a spider's web, sun through beech leaves or the texture of mud squeezed between fingers. The activity boxes in Chapter 1, 'Everyday Places and Spaces', provide examples of activities that help children learn through such 'ecstatic places' (Chawla, 2007).

Having a sense of place, a sense of belonging to a particular corner of the world, impacts on the wellbeing of participants in ways widely known to geographers and anthropologists but less well known generally. Chawla (2007) states that special places are characteristically quiet and peaceful places. They are often places where it is possible to be solitary, all qualities increasingly difficult for many people. Wattchow and Brown (2011: 52) report the impact of the loss of those familiar places before exploring what outdoor education can mean to participants who may be displaced for many different reasons. Louv (2005, 158) explored extending Erikson's attachment theory to nature with the psychologist, and given how important attachment is to mental health this is a powerful argument for exposure to nature on a regular basis.

We may reflect on our own childhoods and the importance in them of special places. These places take time to become important to us but once they are important they hold our memories and create mental markers into adulthood. If we become secure adults then even the destruction of our special place will not destroy its existence or its importance in our minds. The natural world can allow each person to have a special place, and Forest School allows time for the relationship to develop as a part of our spiritual dimension. The changing of the seasons enhances that relationship, heightening our responses to 'our' Forest School site. The first benefit of repeated visits to the same place is, then, a developing sense of place that supports the wellbeing of participants.

The second impact of seasonal changes on participants is that they are seen to respond creatively to seasonal changes, tapping an innate intrinsic need to express themselves. Figure 6.1 shows an adult's response to autumn leaves, and others may choose a similar medium, or may rush around ecstatically shouting, or find tasty words to join together in poetic forms.

Nature has lessons that take time to learn, and the awe and wonder that spring from experiencing seasonal changes at first hand are not replicable and cannot be experienced second hand. This is a spiritual dimension as well as a cognitive one, and feeds into participants' sense of wellbeing, hence the efforts practitioners make to be inclusive and to enable all their charges to get outside (Hopkins, 2011: 127). Watching buds burst on time-lapse photography is amazing, but sensing the weekly changes in the sprouting understory with all five senses is magical.

■ **Figure 6.1** An adult's response to the colours of autumn

PRINCIPLE 2: FOREST SCHOOL TAKES PLACE IN A WOODLAND OR NATURAL WOODED ENVIRONMENT TO SUPPORT THE DEVELOPMENT OF A RELATIONSHIP BETWEEN THE LEARNER AND THE NATURAL WORLD

In his autobiography Jung speaks of the importance of nature to him (Jung, 1963: 49) and the importance of that nature in his concept of religious faith (Jung, 1963: 62). This personal connection has manifested itself in his theories as a recognition of the human connectedness to a collective unconscious that includes nature (Sempik, Hine and Wilcox, 2010: 89). He recognised that trees have a special quality which human beings respond to (Jung, 1963: 86). Others have shared this articulation of the spirituality of trees, which surely echoes our evolutionary past. It is not surprising to find myths and legends from across the world that are centred on trees, some of which have found their way into the major religions of the world. The Norse Yggdrasil, the Buddhist Bo tree and the Islamic Tree of Immortality are but three examples of religious trees. Christian theologians speak of the Tree of Life, and eating the fruit of the tree of knowledge of good and evil was the cause of the fall of man. We tell our children stories of Hansel and Gretel, of Little Red Riding Hood, of forests to hide in, forests to cross, forests where evil lurks. Nimue imprisons Merlin in a tree, variously hawthorn or oak. Shakespeare uses the forest for magical purposes (*A Midsummer Night's Dream*) and as a place of safety to hide in (*As You Like It*). Some of these trees are allegorical representations of aspects of our own nature; some are stories of the powers of the natural world. All tell us that trees are important to us as human beings. Not least, they are important as a key to the management of climate change as they breathe in carbon dioxide and breathe out oxygen whilst securing fragile soils with their roots. Tudge (2005: 369) claims that trees are key to the future of humanity.

Trees are an inspiration to creativity, a balm to a wounded soul and a repository of stories, myths and superstitions, such as passing a child through a tree for healing, described by Deakin (2007: 389). Forest School is rooted in all of this past, and practitioners use it to help participants prepare for the future. Fortunately, when working with the very young it is easy to create the illusion of a wood or forest with very few trees. Many practitioners teach their children to identify an important tree on their way into the wood, and to ask its permission to enter the space. This helps forge the bond between the trees and the children. But even where this is not common practice the children will spontaneously hug the trees and climb them. Chapter 11, 'The Future Outdoors', has an activity box to show how children can interview a tree.

Finding the personality of a tree harks back to our evolutionary animistic past. As our ancestors developed a conscious awareness of their place in the world, and began to try to make sense of it, they imbued the natural world around them with the same consciousness. The Lorelei Rock in Germany is a relic of this animistic past, and there are many others in all countries, natural features that contain a spirit or power in local legend. This animism was the forerunner of the stories, myths and legends already described. Young children use the same processes to make sense of and describe their worlds. A useful phrase to consider is 'ontogenesis echoes phylogenesis': the idea that the development of the individual child follows the same pattern as the development of the species. This is not a water-tight scientific theory, but it does offer some interesting thoughts to reflect on. The idea that each of us carries the memories of the development of the species through the memories of our childhood reminds us of the importance of these early experiences.

Piaget (1926) recognised this as a feature of the preoperational stage of child development, a mode of thought in which inanimate objects are imagined to have life and mental processes. One example is of children playing in a damp wood who noticed that worms were rising to the surface, a response to the vibrations of their running feet. They decided to create a worm sanctuary where they could place rescued worms to save them from being trampled. One girl showed me a particularly fat one that she had christened William. 'I know his name is William because when I said his name he lifted up his head.' Transferring their own capacity for thought and emotion to the worms helped these children to empathise with their plight and encouraged them to care for their welfare. Caring for others, sentient and non-sentient, is a feature of our emotional and spiritual life.

Whilst few adults would subscribe to the same level of animistic transference as is possible in our preoperational phase of development, most adults do hold that capacity to value the life of other living beings as a part of their values and beliefs. Considering Maslow's hierarchy of needs from 1943, we can see that this capacity is only possible when certain conditions have been met. When Forest School practitioners are working with older children and adults whose life-paths have damaged their capacity to move up the hierarchy, and indeed may display unwanted and damaging behaviours, they may use animism to help restore the connections. This echoes the theories behind Nurture Groups (Lucas, Lesley and Buckland, 2014), when practitioners use techniques associated with earlier stages of development to get children's emotional and social development back on track. Forest School practitioners find that this works for older clients, too. In this way the natural world can be allowed in to those people's lives to be a 'natural health service', and the benefits work in both directions. The trees heal the people, and the people protect the trees.

PRINCIPLE 3: FOREST SCHOOL AIMS TO PROMOTE THE HOLISTIC DEVELOPMENT OF ALL THOSE INVOLVED, FOSTERING RESILIENT, CONFIDENT, INDEPENDENT AND CREATIVE LEARNERS

The benefits of this principle build on the aspects I have explored in the previous one, and so I will pick up on some of its themes in that light. For example, it has been over seventy years since Maslow articulated clearly the importance of all aspects of our life experience to the chances of each of us reaching our full potential (Maslow, 1943: 375), but it is still a useful way of thinking about how important it is to take into account the whole person when considering how and what they are taking from an experience. Leach (2013: 5) emphasises the potential of wooded spaces to offer this 'total immersion' (my expression) and the benefits to be accrued. The time that participants can take to reflect and contemplate in Forest School sessions can be deeply spiritual, and it is no surprise that Mindfulness is popular amongst Forest School practitioners. Earth walks are a way in which practitioners may encourage participants to tune into their senses, and sit spots offer a chance to increase awareness of the natural world at a deeper level. All ages can and will gain from these activities in relaxation and meditation, 'improving the participants' spiritual state' (Seekers Wild, 2015). It is important to note here, however, that these are not elements of Forest School initial training and therefore not all practitioners will use them. The ways in which practitioners respond to the holistic needs of their particular participants will come from the interface between the individual practitioner and his/her skills, knowledge and beliefs and those of the participants they are working with. What is common practice is to facilitate holistic interactions with nature to build deeper understandings.

In these ways and in their general approach Forest School practitioners are creating the framework in which participants can be open to the spiritual power of nature. This is not within the context of any particular religion or none, it is simply an acknowledgement that as a species we have spiritual needs and that a holistic experience in a wooded space facilitated by a trained practitioner can enable those needs to be recognised. It enables participants to experience awe and wonder which Gallagher et al. (2015) identify as crucial to scientific as well as creative endeavour, and to creative, artistic success. Such a universal sense must be central to what it means to be human, and is of a higher order than culture, race or creed.

PRINCIPLE 4: FOREST SCHOOL OFFERS LEARNERS THE OPPORTUNITY TO TAKE SUPPORTED RISKS APPROPRIATE TO THE ENVIRONMENT AND TO THEMSELVES

Digby Jones has stated that 'Identifying, understanding and managing risk are essential to progress, economically, socially and culturally' (2007: 6). For the purposes of this chapter it is the last two that are important but if educational establishments aspire to the first then it is appropriate that they should enable those under their guidance to participate in risk-taking activities. Herbert (2010: 128) identifies schools as places dependent on conformism and rule-following, making it difficult to enable children to explore the boundaries of their abilities and stretch them creatively within the classroom walls. More and more schools are turning to Forest School as a way of enabling children to do just that.

It is appropriate to consider that what constitutes risk is culturally embedded. In some countries even very young children have access to sharp adult tools and learn through experience to keep themselves safe, whilst in others the children are protected from all sharp implements until they are approaching maturity. In neither extreme do those children nor the adults they become suffer regular serious injury as the cultures in which they live are predicated on those differences. However, with greater mobility of population between centres of cultural difference resulting in faster changes in societies it may be worth considering some absolutes based on developmental psychology. Most psychological theories embrace the idea that we learn through direct experience. Most psychological theories embrace the idea that creativity is a form of risk-taking. Put these two thoughts together, and one can see why Forest School practitioners believe that it is appropriate to help all children to learn to manage their own safety by learning to evaluate hazards and construct strategies for risk management.

Forest School practitioners will facilitate tool use, fire-lighting and similar activities when they are appropriate to the participants, but these are 'external' risks, the easy observable ones. More subtle are the permissions to take the 'internal' risks, the addicts forming new relationships (Brady, 2011: 192), the teenagers learning to trust themselves (Cree, 2011: 142), the looked-after child opening up to his peers (Wicks, 2011: 158). Young children who choose not to speak indoors do so at Forest School. Children who fail academically succeed outside. These are immensely powerful outcomes when individuals find a space where they feel safe enough to take some very big emotional risks. Through emotional growth and confidence comes spiritual growth and confidence.

Creativity is also predicated on risk-taking (Herbert, 2010: 80). Robinson states that we are all creative, it is just a matter of finding our own field (Robinson, 2001: 3). Many people respond creatively in nature, and find creative solutions to problems when engaging in Forest School activities. Forest School practitioners are trained to encourage just such creativity, even when working with our youngest children. Tim Gill identified four main arguments to support practices that enable children to take developmentally appropriate risks as a part of healthy childhood, and that prepares them for adulthood (Gill, 2007: 15). He continues to promote playful risk-taking in outdoor spaces (Gill, 2014), and as discussed below, the links between play and creativity are well established.

PRINCIPLE 5: FOREST SCHOOL IS RUN BY QUALIFIED FOREST SCHOOL PRACTITIONERS WHO CONTINUOUSLY MAINTAIN AND DEVELOP THEIR PROFESSIONAL PRACTICE

Forest School is led by qualified Forest School practitioners, who are required to hold a minimum of an accredited Level 3 Forest School qualification to lead a group. As can be seen, an experienced Forest School leader needs a minimum level of skill and knowledge across a wide range of areas of expertise, and this rarely happens quickly. Practitioners are encouraged to acknowledge that initial training is like learning to drive a car. Once the practitioner has the licence then they can go out and learn how to drive this magical thing called Forest School. Each practitioner will be stronger in one or more area, and newly qualified practitioners are encouraged to explore where their skill-set will best fit initially. And increasingly there is an expectation that they will engage in continuing professional development (CPD) to develop new skills and expand their knowledge base.

Being aware of the powerful effects of Forest School, particularly when working with older teenagers and adults, is ensuring that the Forest School Association in the UK encourages continual reflective practice as well as CPD.

The training courses approved by the Forest School Association are run by training organisations that are a part of the Forest School Trainer's Network. Details of their activities can be found on the Forest School Association website (www.forestschool association.org/gb-forest-school-trainers-network-and-the-fsa/). They meet regularly to evaluate their courses and decide on improvements. Discussions about whether all practitioners need the same weighting for the different aspects of Forest School delivery is a feature of many of these meetings. Courses may be validated through different awarding bodies but in 2015 the content remained largely the same.

PRINCIPLE 6: FOREST SCHOOL USES A RANGE OF LEARNER-CENTRED PROCESSES TO CREATE A COMMUNITY FOR DEVELOPMENT AND LEARNING

Practitioner observations are an important element of Forest School pedagogy. Initial observations ensure that the Forest School experiences are tailored to learning and development at an individual level. Ongoing observations shape future sessions. Reflective practice is a feature of each session to ensure learners and practitioners can understand their achievements, develop emotional intelligence and plan for the future, and so many sessions incorporate time sitting around the fire pit (whether the fire is lit or not) discussing experiences, preferences and ideas. This element may well be the reason why Forest School is perceived to have had such an impact on the development of communication skills in all the groups it has been tried with. The emphasis on observations, reflections and discussions ensures that (a) all Forest School sessions are different and (b) they are all learner-centred with the participants' interests and needs at the centre of the community of practice.

Regardless of the ages of the participants, play and choice are an integral part of the Forest School learning process, and play is recognised as vital to learning and development at Forest School. As Else says, playing is what we all do to find out about the world about us (Else, 2009: 30). As adults we talk about 'playing' with a new piece of kit to explore its potential. Power (2015) argues for the universality of play and for its place within the pedagogy of Forest School, citing the universality of Sobel's play motifs. And at the 2015 Forest School Conference in the UK Bob Hughes argued for the importance of play at Forest School, for the survival of the species as well as the health of the individual (Hughes, 2012: 81). If it is so important it begs the question 'why do we play?' All animals play to learn and rehearse the skills for life and to establish relationships and bonds or ties. Humans also play in order to explore and to create, amongst other things, and it is an innate drive, an evolutionary tool with a spiritual dimension (Hughes, 2012: 381). As Forest School has a learner-centred pedagogy so its practice necessitates the inclusion of playful activities.

Linked to the importance of play is the importance of storytelling. Observe young children playing and you will hear (and hear before they are fully able to speak the words) a narrative of their play, its story. Listen to a child explaining an event and you can hear them constructing their understanding of the event through the narrative. It is a part of their internal process that is externalised whilst they are inexpert users of language. Once they become more proficient the process is internalised but the stories continue. Our memories are the stories of our past, and the sophistication of our capacity to memorise, to share memories and to apply them to new situations is because we as a species are language users. 'The role of stories in meaning-making is at once personal, social, and cultural' (Gersie, Nanson and Schieffelin, 2014: 47). Story-telling is an integral part of Forest School. It may be sharing stories around a campfire, or relating the session's events, or sharing knowledge about something observed or heard. It may be a way to find an allegory to support the understanding of an event or feeling. It is often a part of the practitioner's mindfulness that will lead them to initiate or support a storytelling activity as a part of the session. Constructing a story is a creative process, and it is an example of what creativity is, namely self-expression and communication. It may also be a spiritual process, an expression of the inner self or a representation of a deep truth about the natural world. Forest School practitioners are sensitive to the power of story and of the need to respect the stories practitioners share with them.

CONCLUSION

This chapter demonstrates how Forest School provides space and time for participants to explore both their spirituality and their creativity through nature, connecting with their inner selves through connecting with the outer wilder world. It offers an alternative to the pressures of modern life for children and adults alike, and a space where we can reclaim the spiritual domain which we need as well as express our creative selves. By doing this in nature there is hope that these adult and child participants will become better able to protect their own wellbeing as well as that of the natural world around them.

REFERENCES

Borradaile, L. (2006) *Forest School Scotland: An Evaluation*. Edinburgh: Forestry Commission Scotland.

Brady, M. (2011) Addicts and Forest School. In Knight, S. *Forest School for All*. London: Sage.

Burls, A. (2007) People and green spaces: promoting public health and mental well-being through ecotherapy. *Journal of Public Mental Health* 6(3): 24–39.

Chawla, L. (2007) Childhood experiences associated with care for the natural world. *Children, Youth & Environments* 17(4): 144–170.3/14

Cree, J. (2011) Maintaining the Forest School ethos while working with 14–19 year old boys. In Knight, S. *Forest School for All*. London: Sage.

Deakin, R. (2007) *Wildwood: A Journey Through Trees*. London: Penguin.

Else, P. (2009) *The Value of Play*. London: Continuum International Publishing Group.

Forest School Association (2015) *Full Principles and Criteria for Good Practice*. www.forestschoolassociation.org/full-principles-and-criteria-for-good-practice/ (accessed 18 October 2015).

Gallagher, S., Janz, B., Reinerman, L., Bockelman, P. and Trempler, J. (2015) *A Neurophenomenology of Awe and Wonder: Towards a Non-Reductionist Cognitive Science*. London: Palgrave MacMillan.

Gersie, A., Nanson, A. and Schieffelin, E. (eds) (2014) *Storytelling for a Greener World: Environment, Community and Story-based Learning*. Stroud: Hawthorn Press.

Gill, T. (2007) *No Fear: Growing Up in a Risk Averse Society*. London: Caloustie Gulbenkian Foundation.

Gill, T. (2014) The benefits of children's engagement with nature: a systematic literature. *Children, Youth and Environments* 24(2), Greening Early Childhood Education, pp. 10–34.

Herbert, A. (2010) *The Pedagogy of Creativity*. London: Routledge.

Hopkins, F. (2011) Removing barriers: getting children with physical challenges into the woods. In Knight, S. (ed.) *Forest School for All*. London: Sage.

Hughes, B. (2012) (2nd edn) *Evolutionary Playwork*. London: Routledge.

Hughes, F. (2007) *Pentre Forest School: An Evaluation of a Forest School Project*. Ruthin: Forestry Commission Wales.

Jones, D. (2007) *Cotton Wool Kids, Issues Paper 7: Releasing the Potential for Children to Take Risks and Innovate*. Coventry: HTI Trust.

Jung, C. (1963) *Memories, Dreams, Reflections*. London: Random House.

Knight, S. (2011) *Risk and Adventure in Early Years Outdoor Play*. London: Sage.

Leach, J. (2013) *Happiness Grows on Trees: How Woodlands Boost Our Wellbeing*. London: Woodlands. Available at: www.woodlands.co.uk/reports (accessed 6 November 2015).

Louv, R. (2005) (2nd edn). *Last Child in the Woods*. London: Atlantic Books.

Lucas, S., Lesley, K. and Buckland, G. (2014) *Nurture Group Principles and Curriculum Guidelines*. London: The Nurture Group Network. Available at: www.nurturegroups.org/publications/theory-practice/nurture-group-principles-and-curriculum-guidelines (accessed 9 November 2015).

Maslow, A. (1943) *A Theory of Human Motivation*. Originally published in *Psychological Review*, 50, 370–396. Available at: www.simplypsychology.org/maslow.html (accessed 6 November 2015).

Natural England (2009) *Our Natural Health Service*. London: Natural England. Available at: www.naturalengland.org.uk/publications (accessed 6 November 2015).

Natural England (2010) *A Manifesto for the Natural Environment*. London: Natural England. Available at: www.naturalengland.org.uk/publications (accessed 6 November 2015).

O'Brien, L. and Murray, R. (2007) Forest School and its impacts on young children: case studies in Britain. *Urban Forestry & Urban Greening* 6: 249–265.

Piaget, J. (1926) *The Child's Conception of the World*. Trans. Totowa, NJ: Rowman and Allanheld (1960). Originally published as *La représentation du monde chez l'enfant*. Paris: Presses Universitaires de France.

Power, M. (2015) Lost in translation or still being translated? Reflections on the Forest and Nature School Movement in Canada. *Pathways: The Ontario Journal of Outdoor Education,* Spring, 27(3).

Robinson, K. (2001) *Out of Our Minds: Learning to Be Creative*. Chichester: Capstone Publishing.

Seekers Wild (2015) *The 5 W's of Sit Spots*. Available at: www.seekerswild.com/sit-spot.html (accessed 6 November 2015).

Sempik, J., Hine R. and Wilcox, D. (eds) (2010) *Green Care: A Conceptual Framework, A Report of the Working Group on the Health Benefits of Green Care*, COST Action 866, Green Care in Agriculture. Loughborough: Centre for Child and Family Research, Loughborough University.

Tudge, C. (2005) *The Secret Life of Trees: How They Live and Why They Matter*. London: Penguin.

Vining, J., Merrick, M. and Price, E. (2008) The distinction between humans and nature: human perceptions of connectedness to nature and elements of the natural and unnatural. *Human Ecology Review* 15(1).

Wattchow, B. and Brown, M. (2011) *A Pedagogy of Place: Outdoor Education for a Changing World*. Victoria, Australia: Monash University Publishing.

Wicks, R. (2011) Forest School and looked after children. In Knight, S. *Forest School for All*. London: Sage.

Wilson, E.O. (1984) *Biophilia*. Cambridge, MA: Harvard University Press.

BEACH SCHOOLS

Margaret Mackintosh

INTRODUCTION

Schools in or near coastal settlements are fortunate in having the wonderful resource that provides the opportunity to create a *beach school* within their reach. This chapter seeks to explore the ways in which children can learn through coastal environments, with an emphasis on beach schools, as part of their whole school curriculum. However, it is important to note that many of the activities, ideas and thinking within this chapter can be applied to many different schools and environments, and to occasional trips to the coast as well as to regular visits.

Beach schools are a development from Forest Schools, with a shared ethos and philosophy centred on children's social, emotional, mental and physical health as well as intellectual development. Much has been written about the relationship between leisure environments, access to and use of natural spaces, health and well-being. Most refers to forests and woodland, but the arguments presented are just as relevant for coasts and beaches. And most refers to adults, but it is just as relevant to children, since contact with nature can extend a positive influence on the physical and mental health of human beings in their increasingly urbanised lives (Tabbush and O'Brien 2002).

Many Forest School ideas and activities in addition to shelter-building, such as fire lighting, cooking, games and story-telling, can be transferred to the beach environment. For example, one teacher commented on how excited she was when children, transferring their forest shelter-building to the beach, realised that they could weigh the tarpaulin edge down with sand and large pebbles to stop it flapping and lifting in the strong wind. But the coast also offers its own unique opportunities for creative activity; one only has to consider the differences between children peering under logs to look for woodlice and deep into rock pools to look for crabs. Coastlines hold a wealth of opportunities for informal and more formal learning and teaching. The landscape is unique, the excitement walking down to a beach is unique and the very air that we breathe down by the sea is unique.

THE BEACH

When primary children are taken to the beach from school it's often for geography fieldwork. Depending on their age and experience, in geography children would learn about some human features at the coast, including settlement, fishing, docks, ports and tourist

BOX 7.1 A WORD ON SAFETY

With its proximity to water, taking children to the beach involves encountering a unique set of hazards, so consulting tide tables for time and height of high and low tides and checking wind direction is essential. As well as being prepared for dealing with waves, tides, rock pools and cliffs, teachers need to be aware that sections of coast may be protected by landscape or nature conservation designations such as Area of Outstanding Natural Beauty (AONB) and Site of Special Scientific Interest (SSSI), and that the National Trust manages and preserves lengths of coastline.

resorts, and some physical features including rock pools, wildlife, cliffs, beach, dunes, sea, tides, often a river mouth or estuary. But this is frequently for a one-off or possibly annual or residential fieldtrip. A beach school is an all-year-round resource, offering so much more during the children's many visits throughout the year, so many opportunities for play, fun, enjoyment and teamwork as well as stimuli for or illustration of cross-curricular work, particularly art, English, music, science, history and including geography.

THE BEACH IS ALWAYS HERE!

A Year Five boy from Birmingham, visiting the coast for the first time on a sunny summer's day, looked up and down the expanse of golden sands and asked 'Is it still here in winter?' Do many children similarly perceive that beaches are just for summer? How many primary school children actually experience UK beaches? Explore a class's travel experiences and you'll probably find that, unfortunately, many of those lucky enough to have holidays tend to visit overseas swimming pools surrounded by modern hotels in hot, sunny weather.

There's an oft-repeated expression that 'there's no such thing as inappropriate weather, just inappropriate clothing'. Experience suggests that, as long as they do have appropriate clothing, children enjoy going to the beach in rough, wet, windy, even cold, weather. Feeling a strong wind on their faces and watching big waves breaking on the shore, sea wall or rocks can be valuable experiential learning in its own right. Some teachers report that the children actually prefer the adventure of bad weather days – getting out and walking and building up resilience – because they are often denied this opportunity by understandably protective parents who fear the effects such weather might have on their children's health!

THE SETTING

Several primary schools in Exmouth, UK have established different models of beach schools. Two of these will be used for exemplification in this chapter, with readers being able to extract relevant ideas and adapt them to their own situation.

Exmouth is a small town (population c. 35,000) on the East Devon coast, at the mouth of the River Exe. The estuary is a very special environment and is an internationally important site for wildlife, particularly for migrating birds. In addition to the town itself, the seaside resort has beautiful beaches, cliffs, rock pools, a marina, RNLI station and

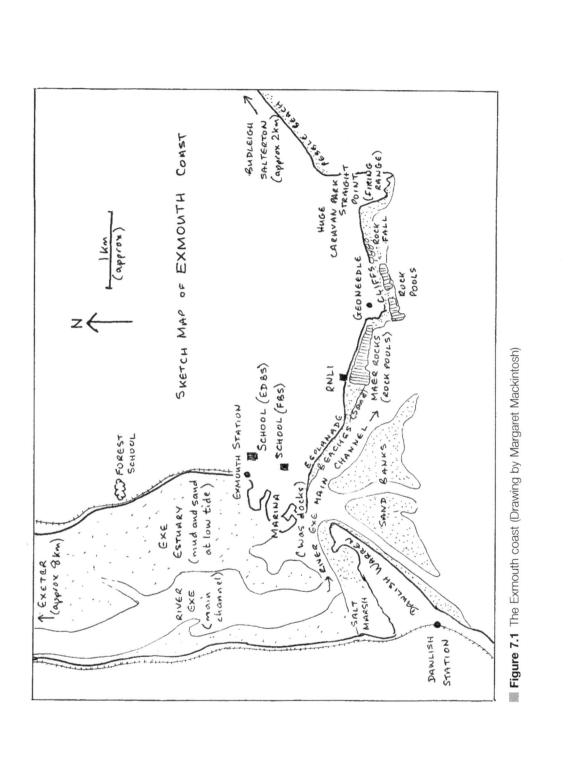

Figure 7.1 The Exmouth coast (Drawing by Margaret Mackintosh)

other interesting features. This location therefore enjoys many different features for school groups to explore and learn from.

ORGANISATION OF BEACH SCHOOL

To gain most benefit from a Beach School, as with a Forest School, children should visit and learn there throughout the year. One Exmouth school opens its Beach School all year to their Y3 pupils. The class teacher who has a beach school qualification (from Archimedes), and at least five other adults, accompany the whole class to a sandy beach and rock pool location near the RNLI station every Friday afternoon (except when this would be dangerous, usually when high tides and strong SW winds coincide). The school rents a small beach hut for storage. Other locations are also used, such as the cliff top path and the marina, when resources from the hut are not needed. At this school other classes enjoy regular 'focused' visits and the Reception/Foundation class spends an afternoon at the beach fortnightly throughout the Spring and Summer terms in their first year in school. The younger children tend to use it more in winter, keeping moving as they play group and team games on the beach, developing social skills, gaining experiences and a love of the outdoors. In the summer with, hopefully, warmer weather, the older pupils enjoy visits where they can engage in more extended and possibly more 'academic' group and team activities and data and resource collection while still maintaining the fun element. So, as they progress through the school, children's blocked experience of beach school moves through the seasons.

The school uses a range of locations from the estuary, round the marina, along the esplanade, past the RNLI station and rock pools to the cliffs and cliff path where the Geoneedle at the western end of the Jurassic Coast World Heritage Site provides a good vantage point to get a view over the stretch of coast to both east and west. An elevated point that offers the opportunity to look down on the coastal environment is a real asset.

■ **Figure 7.2** Crossing the river

The beach school agenda is tailored by the class teacher to fit in with the curriculum. And invariably the children return from the beach full of ideas and the next ten are buzzing to go. These schools are particularly lucky with the variety of coastal environments on their doorstep, but it does not take much creativity to make super use of almost any safe, coastal environment.

STARTING WITH PLAY

The school initially opened beach (and Forest) school as an intervention for children with behavioural, mental, emotional and/or social issues, but quickly extended it to all children once its value was appreciated. The children express a preference for beach school where, incidentally, they demonstrate greater use of language and improved place or memory imprinting.

As described above, the ethos and philosophy of beach (and forest) schools is centred on children's social, emotional, mental and physical health as well as intellectual development. Play, therefore, has a central role in beach school visits. While they enjoy and explore the coastal environment the children are relaxing, having fun, sharing experiences with other children, co-operating and engaging in team games and getting to know each other. They make and develop friendships in an out-of-school situation; something which is very important for all children, not least of all those who live in otherwise isolated situations at home. Many of them engage in activities at the beach that they have not previously been able to do, for a variety of reasons, and in doing so develop a great range of social and cognitive skills. As a teacher for example, you could set creative sand-sculpture challenges, because sand can be used for so much more than making sand castles with! Or if you are a traditionalist why not set competitive castle building challenges? The children will learn to work cooperatively in building and decorating a huge castle with a moat, excavating streams and rivers, constructing dams, watching the tide come in to fill the moat and river, being disappointed as erosion collapses their structures – so much fun, but with an 'educational' pay-off. Activities such as these, involving design technology and science (materials), provide opportunities for cooperation and learning to manage failure, develop resilience and celebrate success. This can be drawn on back in school, as the children talk about their visit to beach school, possibly aided by digital photographs of the activities.

WAKING UP ALL THE SENSES

As beach schools' potential to support classroom work, including art work and the collection of resources, has become more explicit, teachers admit to having become more adventurous in their planning. They show very high commitment to the initiative and comment that it 'wakes up all the senses', with the children always coming back smiling.

Andy Goldsworthy, Sir Antony Gormley and Richard Long are three artists whose work is introduced in the classroom and powerfully explored at the beach.

AT BEACH SCHOOL WITH SIR ANTONY GORMLEY

Sir Antony Gormley is a British sculptor probably best known for his huge 'Angel of the North' (1998) at Gateshead, in Tyne and Wear. He also created 'Another Place' (1997),

■ **Figures 7.3 and 7.4** Gormley sculptures on the beach

(Photograph with permission: Mark Riley, Creative States)

now permanently located at Crosby Beach near Liverpool. It consists of a hundred cast iron sculptures of Gormley's body, facing towards the sea.

In an interview for the *Liverpool Echo* Gormley said that, although the installation was meant to travel around, Crosby is excellent as a permanent home because of its history, the history of Liverpool docks and everything that came in and went out of them. He also revealed that the original piece was designed in a way as a meditation on emigration and what drove human beings constantly to expand westwards until finally they reached the Californian Pacific. What a fantastic idea to get children creating their own images, or any art installations really, to represent their thoughts on current issues and topics. And sand sculptures have the additional talking point of being ephemeral.

Having talked about, and possibly had a chance to practise meditation in school, encourage each child to become a sensory statue by finding a space and standing, still and alone, facing the sea, like one of Gormley's statues. With older pupils it might be appropriate, at the present time, to think about immigration and refugees as well as emigration. But all children can be asked to think about what they can see, as they gaze, unmoving, out to sea. What can they hear and smell? What do they feel, literally and emotionally? What words come to mind? Talk about the experience while still at beach school, but encourage children to recall and record responses later with speech bubbles on a digital photograph of the human 'sculptures'.

AT BEACH SCHOOL WITH ANDY GOLDSWORTHY

Andy Goldsworthy is a sculptor, photographer and environmentalist who works with nature, using petals, flowers, leaves, twigs and stones, amongst other found materials. Children enjoy cooperating to make group sculptures from found materials – seaweed, feathers, shells – and materials discarded by people, like plastic and rope, found on the strand line. This fun activity alerts children to materials available at the beach and also to human impact on the environment. What do they think, and what can be done, about our litter? Is it harmful to wildlife, people, the environment? There is a golden opportunity here to address the issue of, for example, plastics in the oceans and turn anger or sadness amongst the children into positive, creative action. Children can make real links between the rubbish they find on the beaches and their own responsibilities to look after our local environment. Links can be made through geography to design and technology, English and maths.

AT BEACH SCHOOL WITH RICHARD LONG

Richard Long is an English sculptor particularly well known for his land art and text-works or word art. Both these genres lend themselves to beach school since his artworks are frequently created on walks, often epic walks in wild landscapes. For his land art, Long deliberately changes the environment in some way, creating sculptures using materials found in the immediate locality, particularly rocks and stones. Sometimes he removes material, clearing spaces, but he never damages the environment.

A walk along a stretch of beach or estuary provides another sculpture opportunity, a chance for children to create a 'Long' sculpture from found materials – rock, pebbles, shells, seaweed or driftwood. As an individual activity children could be encouraged to express the emotions invoked by beach school, or as a small group activity the focus could be on teamwork and cooperation.

Some children walking along the beach in Orkney created some land art in response to their visit to the adjacent Neolithic archaeological site at Skara Brae, others made a group sculpture on an Outer Hebrides beach, using natural materials and discarded rubbish

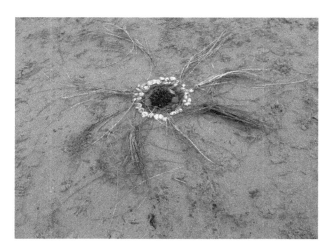

Figures 7.5 and 7.6 Children's art inspired by Andy Goldsworthy

Figure 7.9 Recreating an ancient Scottish settlement at Skara Brae, using natural materials as well as rubbish found on the beach

■ **Figure 7.10** Stone sculptures created by children at Skara Brae

– a tyre and coat hanger. Another group cooperated to make a ring of standing stones on the rocky beach at Lyme Regis. Unfortunately, although being well along the beach away from the town, this was vandalised – there's a lesson!

FROM SCULPTURE TO WORDS

In addition to creating sculptures, Long sometimes records his response to the landscape as textworks. He uses words about place, locality, time, distance and measurement (Figure 7.7). This is an activity children might enjoy exploring, after looking at examples of Long's work. Encourage them to create textworks as, or after, they walk along the coast, perhaps on the beach, perhaps on a cliff path or beside an estuary. Do they include words expressing their feelings, or do they limit their word or text art to factual description, starting and finishing points, time, tides?

The teacher commented on how much the children enjoyed beach art, finding it relaxing, and that engaging with beach sculpture helped them appreciate that art is much more than painting. The children realised that 'it's for everybody and you can do it with anything'. Another teacher remarked that art is how people, including children, make sense of their location. How they choose to illustrate the positives and negatives helps them decide what is, and is not, significant. This will have relevance when children create and use maps. What have map-makers included and left out?

BEACH SCHOOLS AND THE CURRICULUM

There are so many examples of activities for children to do at beach schools and so I have set out just a few examples that I have experienced. The basic line, I suppose, is to be guided by a balance between the children's ideas and links that can be made to their current learning in as wide a range of subject areas as possible.

In pairs Year Three children drew clocks in the sand and practised time telling. Small groups drew and labelled skeletons. Can children recreate in sand, or with natural materials, the skeletons and shapes of the creatures that they find on the beach (or even the creatures they imagine may once have lived here)? From a vantage point, in this case the cliff-top Geoneedle at the western end of the Jurassic Coast, they looked down on the coast and described what they could see. The children pointed out how the colours of the rocks in the cliff changed and layered like a big cake, and they spotted the effect of waves and tides that had created patterns in the sand. The children looked at and considered the location of, and relationship between, the town, the estuary and Dawlish Warren. Walking along the cliff path to the next small town, Budleigh Salterton, they saw at first hand the effects of cliff erosion. They designed a sand city on the beach and discussed the 'best location' for schools, churches and shops.

The Year Three class were completing a topic on South America and so it seemed only natural to them to create sand sculptures of Aztec temples, and then to engage in Aztecan role play – although fortunately no child was sacrificed to the God of the rains! Later followed an activity that the children saw as fun but the teacher saw as summative assessment! In groups, they created impressive 3-D maps of South America in the sand (Figure 7.11). Teamwork was needed for decision-making as they agreed to use pebbles and sand mountains to 'build' the Andes along the west coast, flattening the tops with sand to create a plateau. Bobbly bladderwrack seaweed – great fun to burst the 'air bubbles' – was chosen to represent rainforest, lengths of kelp seaweed became rivers and shells located cities. The children were impressively creative in their map-making in a way that could not have happened in the classroom, and adjustments could easily be made. Throughout all this they were gaining, in an informal setting, a greater understanding of the materials of the coast.

PATTERNS IN THE SAND

As well as classes visiting regularly there is much to be gained from an occasional visit, too. The Reception children made one such visit. While Tim Peake was at the International Space Station (ISS) they were talking, sharing their ideas and learning about the moon, the Earth and space. When they went to the beach they initially had fun playing throwing games. Afterwards they threw balls of different sizes and weights up high and watched them land on the sand in a defined area. They saw craters and space debris created on impact, resembling photos they had seen of the surface of the moon. It was very exciting and memorable, helping the children to make sense of the moon and craters and also to demonstrate gravity. Such learning helps to forge a bridge to future learning.

ESTUARY PATTERNS

The idea of pattern can also be explored in the mud, sand, pebbles and shells of the estuary at low tide and in the rocks of the cliffs or foreshore. Recognition of pattern is so important in maths and science. Identification of patterns at the coast leads to speculation of how they are formed. This can be assisted by watching the flow of water in the river and on the in-coming and out-going tides. An estuary is a good place to watch tidal movements as the water drains out or creeps in, with the direction of flow is usually very clear.

■ **Figure 7.11** Making a map of South America (Drawing by Margaret Mackintosh)

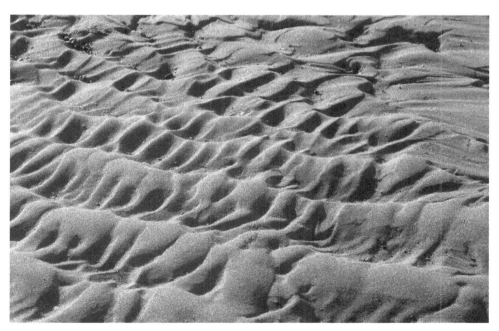

■ **Figure 7.12** Sand ripples

▨ **Figure 7.13** Rock patterns

There is abundant wildlife in an estuary to observe, photograph, identify, celebrate and ask 'why is it here?', leading to the idea of environmental niches. There are sea birds, especially waders, flying over and feeding in the rich environment, prompting 'what are they eating?' There are shellfish (cockles, mussels, razor shells, winkles, whelks) on and in the mud, fascinating sand mason worms and large worms (ragworms and lugworms) dug up to be used as bait for fishing. Many of these creatures leave footprints or trails which are fun to follow, but children will enjoy making their own footprint patterns. It may be possible to speak to a bait digger who will have tales to tell about the estuary. There are small fish, crabs and other life on pebble banks in the estuary, indeed lots of wildlife to find and celebrate. This environment and the wildlife favouring it can be compared with the rockpools elsewhere on the shore.

FROM RIVER TO SEA

For children the beach is an entity in itself. An end-point if you like, or the line around the edge of the country. However the coastal zone actually blends into the landscape behind it through physical features such as streams and rivers as well as human features as a coastal town smudges the distinction between the coast and 'inland'. In other words children should not be encouraged to see the beach in isolation but as part of a changing landscape. It helps, for example, to walk the children through a coastal town down to the seaside. It becomes clear how humans interact with and impact on the physical landscape in this way.

The children at Exmouth have commented on how their legs had ached when they started going to beach school, but that they no longer do! Doing these walks has enabled the children to connect their school to beach and estuary and the town to beach. As they realise how different parts of their environment connect to each other they are contextualising their school in their seaside location, building a 3-D understanding of coastal Exmouth. They are also developing an understanding of how different environments have different outcomes, to weather, human activity, to and for wildlife and more. This is all contributing, in a most enjoyable and memorable way, to their understanding of place on a range of scales, from small rock pool to whole town. This was referred to earlier as 'improved place or memory imprinting'. Back in the classroom GoogleEarth/satellite images are useful, especially as a bridge towards an understanding of maps.

CHANGE ON MANY SCALES

Tidal change has already been mentioned, but there are many other changes for the children to experience, on a range of scales – movement of the sand, waves, weather, seasonal, number of visitors, use of beach throughout the year, even presence or absence of seaweed. Like many seaside towns and resorts, Exmouth is about to undergo redevelopment and a major change. Walking from one end of the coast to the other, from the marina to the cliffs at Orcombe Point and then 'back over the top' via the vantage point of the Geoneedle, provides the older children with an excellent view of the area to be changed. As the plans are contentious the children are very ready to engage in the arguments. They have their opinions and they readily debated the new development plans (available in the local newspaper) and engaged enthusiastically in persuasive writing, with letters that presented a balanced argument to their MP. A real situation for using the skills gained in the classroom and at beach school.

In addition to future change, children enjoy looking at photographs (old postcards, for example) and paintings of what places were like in the past. Encourage them to identify the location where the photographs were taken, to take a photo of the views today and to comment on the changes. Do they consider them to be improvements? Why were the changes made or necessary? Why did the docks become a marina? This leads to investigating the history of the town that can be enriched by interviews with elderly residents. There might even be tales of pirates, local historical characters, possibly even back to Roman times. There might be a blue plaque trail, or children might enjoy creating a history trail from their discoveries. Lots of scope for imagination, adventure and drama! What would some of the ancient locals, who happened to have been transported magically from their homes some one, two or even eight hundred years into their future, and our present, to talk to us today think of the changes they see before them?

LISTENING TO THE SEA – AND TO EACH OTHER

Year Four and Five pupils have found the beach to be a great location for performance poetry. Each group of children chose from a selection of poems and worked on their performance. The other children then became the audience and the show was filmed on iPads for working on later. And from here there is a natural progression to move on to writing their own poems. Teachers have commented on better 'engagement', especially among the boys, and that finding their own spaces is important. At beach school there isn't the feeling of being 'trapped' like there can be in the classroom. Attention has been maintained for up to an hour and tasks have been successfully completed in good time. The relaxed atmosphere of the beach can bring inspiration, emotion and success, a feeling of well-being.

SCIENCE AT THE MARINA

A marina with fishing boats and yachts is an ideal and interesting place to observe pulleys and levers in use, and to learn the appropriate vocabulary. Groups of children were set the task of creating a mechanism to lift their TA. They were given the design clue that they would need to build a lever, using anything they wanted to, and the word 'fulcrum' was mentioned. They succeeded.

Links with fishing boats having been made, in this context buoys, navigation, compass work, bearings of landmarks and some mapwork were introduced for older pupils, although you may prefer to stick to satellite images at this stage.

Linked with compass work, instructions to create shapes, patterns and pictures on the beach, combining number of footsteps, directions and angles, have proven to be great fun for small groups.

ROCK POOLS

Children love exploring rock pools, but unfortunately many have not had the chance to enjoy it, unlike these lucky eight year olds (Figure 7.14). Crabbing on a rocky beach in Cornwall he told me I wouldn't find Velvet Crabs where I was looking – 'they don't live in that sort of place'. He was beginning to show an understanding of ecological niches! As rock pooling is a standard activity at the beach, there's no need to go into detail here, just to mention the range of flora and fauna that can be found, the opportunities for photography and sketching and to use identification charts. A child sees a rock pool from one perspective, peering down into the watery depths – but what would a crab see, looking back up? Encourage the children to write poetry from the perspective of a sea anemone or a limpet, or a crab.

Rock pooling provides a good bridge to marine ecology and conservation, coastal management, sustainability and climate change, especially if linked with careful (Health & Safety) exploration of the marine and human 'treasures' of strand lines and the need for human responsibility in an environment shared by people and wildlife. It is not too big a leap for children to be able to see a rock pool as a 'mini-world' for those that live within it. It is not a closed eco-system by any means (particularly when the tide starts to come in), but in caring for a rock pool children can understand more clearly the need for them to care for the World. They gaze into a mini-world.

BEACH GAMES

Every teacher will have a repertoire of bat, ball and rope games that are great in the open space of a beach, but two particularly popular at the beach schools I have experienced are the Rope Game and the Octopus Game. They both require cooperation, communication and team work. In the rope game all children stand outside a circular rope, pick it up to waist level and pull it. Unless they cooperate, the ring collapses and they all fall down.

■ **Figure 7.14** Children exploring rockpools

The Octopus Game is slightly more challenging. A ball is placed on a plate with a lip to which eight strings are attached (or one for each child). The challenge is to lift up the plate without the ball falling out. The children have to cooperate and all pull together to succeed. Give the children free time to organise their own games, or to create games to teach and show to other groups. Give a group of children the challenge of creating a game for another group to play that involves teamwork to succeed, or ball skills, or . . . whatever else you would like to encourage. And of course the children's favourite is invariably 'Capture the Flag'. Great fun for all!

CONCLUSION

Throughout this chapter the focus has been on using fun activities and play for health, well-being and learning, and for creating 'bridges' so that when children meet something (possibly new) in the classroom, now and in the future, they say 'Oh yes, I remember . . .' and conjure up images from their beach school experiences. Building castles, digging holes, creating streams, rivers, dams and watching the incoming tide inundate them all help the children create these 'bridges' to later learning and model what happens on a larger scale in the landscape, in a fun and playful setting.

It is well established that children learn through play – adults do too! When we get a new kitchen or garage gadget, car, camera, phone or tablet what do we do first? Play with it. The decline in opportunities for children to find time and space for play has been linked with concerns about children's physical and mental health, including obesity and lack of independence. 'Adult-organised and purposeful activity . . . may run counter to children's desire to play with peers in spontaneous, opportunistic and unpredictable forms (Lester and Russell, 2008, 2010). These concerns are addressed by beach (and forest) school, especially since outdoor contexts with low-level adult presence and control, enabling freedom for children to engage in sustained inter-child play and interaction, has been shown to lead to social cohesion in the classroom and to contribute to social development and learning (Waite et al., 2013).

With beach school open all year, your priority will be to ensure that the children are warm and are well prepared with the correct clothing, have healthy snacks and drinks with them and, most of all, feel physically and emotionally safe.

Although you will seek to inspire them the children will, undoubtedly, inspire you with their creativity, awe and wonder, and their enjoyment of the coast. Fostering their emerging respect for, and understanding of, the beach and the sea should lead to lifelong awareness of how delicate, and in need of careful sustainable management, our local environments are.

However you utilise beaches for outdoor play and learning, each beach school site is unique; you design it to meet the needs of your group and to fit the environment you are working in, but your purpose will be the same. You will want to utilise the challenges offered by the outdoor environment to develop children's social, spiritual, emotional, mental and physical health. You will want to use in-school skills and subject learning in different ways outdoors, and bring outdoor experiences into the classroom. You will want children to enhance their self-reliance, communication and cooperation, but most of all you will want them to relax, to play and have fun as they learn in the outdoors.

With thanks to:

▨ Felicity Tetley, Y3 teacher, Beacon VA C of E Primary School
▨ Sue Lockwood, Head, Beacon VA C of E Primary School
▨ Martin Clarke, HLTA, Exeter Road Community Primary School
▨ Paul Gosling, Head, Exeter Road Community Primary School

REFERENCES

Lester, S. and Russell, W. (2008) *Play for a Change: Play, Policy and Practice – A Review of Contemporary Perspectives*. London, National Children's Bureau.

Lester, S. and Russell, W. (2010) *Children's Right to Play: An Examination of the Importance of Play in the Lives of Children Worldwide*. The Hague, Bernard van Leer Foundation.

Tabbush, P. and O'Brien, L. (2002) *Health and Well-being: Trees, Woodlands and Natural Spaces*. Edinburgh, Forestry Commission.

Waite, S., Rogers, S. and Evans, J. (2013) Freedom, flow and fairness: exploring how children develop socially at school through outdoor play. *Journal of Adventure Education & Outdoor Learning*, 13 (3), 255–276.

CHAPTER 8

CURIOUS EXPLORATIONS

Jane Whittle

INTRODUCTION

Teachers are in the wonderful position of being able to foster children's awe and wonder about the outdoors. They have the opportunity to help children make sense of their enquiries and to observe patterns in nature whilst providing time for pupils to sit, lie or sink into outdoor spaces to wonder and wander. The aim for teachers is to support pupils to make personal attachments to the outdoors and to ignite a spark for life-long curiosity towards spaces and places. Teachers can observe the natural curiosity children have for physical spaces and support their discoveries about how these places may change over time. Through outdoor learning, pupils begin to understand how patterns and processes shape our world. An ideal location to explore this connection is a river site. In enquiring into rivers, pupils see the outdoors in action and within a river system there is a huge wealth of processes to be explored. Because of this, rivers have the potential to engage pupils across the entire curriculum. Rivers are used as an example here, although really the local environment is full of both natural and human processes and features that can be used for creative approaches to learning. Curious explorations can happen in a wide range of environments. Rivers are themselves creative in the way they move through landscapes. Whether you are at the source of a river or standing on the bank of a river's meander, there is something special and unique to investigate. So what better way to foster creativity in pupils than supporting them to think creatively about processes and patterns from a variety of curricular perspectives? Creativity is born out of curiosity and because rivers are complex, living features there is much to be curious about. This chapter aims to outline a range of activities which could spark interest in pupils to think creatively, act creatively and reflect on this in creative ways. The activities aim to span the different modes of creativity outlined by Desailly (2015, p.4):

Being creative involves:

- Generating new ideas
- Synthesising a variety of other people's ideas into a new understanding
- Reflection and evaluation
- Finding patterns

■ Researching
■ Hypothesising
■ Generalising
■ Being investigative and enquiring
■ Reaching conclusions.

The activities aim to integrate these ways into creativity and encourage teachers to work alongside pupils and support their enquiries. As Taylor states, 'outdoor learning offers us a way to build the foundations for creativity for all children' (2012, p.122), and investigating a river promotes differentiation in many areas such as learning styles, academic ability and thinking skills. Each pupil in the class will come to lessons with a varied understanding of rivers depending on their own experiences, and taking time to explore this prior to embarking on the following activities will ensure all pupils are encouraged to develop their curiosity. The terms 'river work' and 'fieldwork' suggest geography to many teachers and it is true that there are wonderful and creative geographical activities and learning to be gained from field and river work activities; but geographers are not the sole beneficiaries of river work and field work. Rivers can provide a vast array of cross-curricular opportunities for learning.

PLANNING FOR RIVERS WORK

Prior to embarking on planning, it is important to decide the focus of the river fieldwork. Rivers are an exciting cross-curricular tool and therefore teachers might begin by considering the following questions:

■ Is the learning outcome specific to one stand-alone subject or might pupils approach the fieldwork from multiple subject perspectives?
■ Do the pupils require specific curriculum knowledge prior to the visit?
■ Is the fieldwork appropriate for cross-curricular work?
■ Will children have the opportunity to be creative and use their imagination?
■ Are the outcomes of the outdoor learning to be defined by the teacher or will they grow out of the fieldwork?

Deciding when to plan a visit to the river will depend on the purpose of the fieldwork. If you are fortunate to have a site in your locality, weekly visits could really help to develop the range of activities explored in this chapter. Beginning a unit of work with a field visit could inspire pupils and is a unique way to encourage pupils to create enquiry questions. Completing fieldwork at the mid-point of a unit allows pupils to test theories and develop their understanding further and they can return to the classroom with evidence to add to their learning. Saving the field visit to the end of a unit allows pupils to plan and develop their ideas and may be a useful conclusion to the unit of work. When making the decision on when and duration, it would be helpful to consider the connection you are aiming for between the fieldwork and the work in the classroom. If seen as a 'prize' at the end of the unit, pupils will not benefit from the explorations and will take less from the experience. Robertson (2014, p.160) explains that 'if outdoor sessions work in harmony with indoor activities, and vice versa, this can be helpful in terms of enabling children to make connections and transfer skills into different contexts.'

Continuing the Speed measuring...

Here are some photos of us measuring:

In my opinion this was a somewhat effective way of measuring the speed because maybe we weren't so accurate at throwing the apple or at measuring the 10 metre string because perhaps the apple could have been thrown in front of the person holding the string instead of throwing it in line with the person holding the string and the string was not exactly 10 metres because some of the string was used to be wrapped around the apple. I might have pulled the string towards me without noticing it and this could have effected the results.

Figure 8.1 Children working out how to measure the speed of the river

Table 8.1 A range of curriculum activities to enhance an appreciation of the world around us

Language
Report writing based on investigations and enquiry led activities
Persuasive writing from the point of view of the river or in terms of action that could be taken relating to the sustainability of the river
Poetry writing based on the features and processes at the river
Labelling and annotating skills through sketches and app work
Narrative writing based on wildlife at the river site or use of the river as the narrative setting
Development of talk around rivers concepts, systems and processes
Drama based work through role plays at the river site, leading to play-script work
Research using non-fiction books and film

Mathematics
Data collection methods and analysis of data including comparison work
Use of measuring tools to measure and understand the river
Use of mathematical vocabulary to make sense of physical processes
Application of work on angles, possibly through the use of apps
Use of conversions in speed and distance
Use of statistical data to enquire into the river
Shape hunting as a means of finding 2D and 3D shapes and patterns in the environment
Development of one-to-one correspondence when counting objects
Creative development of measuring devices, planned and made by pupils

Sciences
Sampling and collecting data through the use of quadrants and other scientific materials
Use of scientific vocabulary to describe habitats and nature at the river site
Discussion of the overlap between geography and science in helping us to understand the world
Investigating pollution at a river through pH indicators
Understanding the effects of pollution on a natural space
Planning and carrying out of investigations with a fair test in mind
Understanding the 5 senses are a tool for observation

Humanities
Investigation of the river's past through photographs, maps and local museum artefacts
Considering the change to rivers over time (both seasonal and annually)
Enquiring into aerial photographs, digital maps and non-fiction texts
Understanding river processes and the places they move through
Debating the flood prevention schemes and researching their effectiveness
Use of observation to understand more about the river processes
Notion of the river as a creative source for stories about beliefs

Arts
Creating landscape drawings using local materials as the paint pallet
Using colour wheels to identify the colours in nature
Using tracing overlays to observe different aspects of the river to develop a more complex artistic interpretation
Investigation of instruments which effectively replicate the river's sound
Selecting musical clips which denote the different features of a river and could accompany written work such as poetry

Design and technology
Creating replicas of flood defences to explain how they might be effective
Designing and making rafts and flotation devices to move objects along a river
Use of apps to annotate images at the river or to take formal measurements
Use of film to capture events and actions at the river to be narrated back in the classroom
Use of geocaches to collect and store data
Capturing observations through digital cameras
Creation of apps to record and detail experiences at the river site

PSE
Use of Philosophy for Children to create debate and inspire action
Bringing the river to life through conceptual lenses thus promoting critical thinking skills
Development of team work through collaborative activities and challenges
Consideration towards the Countryside Code and risk-benefit assessments

Physical education
Orienteering along the river site
Walking a distance of the river, challenging fitness levels at steeper points
Creating the river features through dance or movement
Use of Total Physical Response to explain river processes
Consideration of spatial awareness and balance when moving in shallow waters

Effective outdoor experiences, which may lead to learning, will invite pupils to use their senses, incorporate practical experiences into their thinking and begin to be more critical of information they accessed in class. In taking a river site as a focus, pupils will need to draw on skills from across the curriculum. The aim of the outdoor learning experience is to improve and extend understanding and in asking pupils to take aspects of their prior learning across the curriculum they begin to see how a range of subjects can be used to help them make sense of a place. Pupils who are able to do this independently and select from a bank of skills will be showing creativity in that they will be choosing the most effective skill to suit their investigations.

The activities suggested in Table 8.1 and expanded upon below aim to develop pupils' existing skills and enhance pupils' appreciation of the world around them. They move away from traditional teaching of fieldwork and allow the pupils to explore their own ways of investigating a river and develop a broader sense of the outdoors. Most encourage points of reflection throughout the process to develop evaluative thinking and a notion of critical appraisal of creative ideas. Through analysing these reflections teachers can assess what pupils have learnt from the outdoors experience.

RIVERS THROUGH THE FEET

Pupils need time to engage with a place rather than launching straight into an investigation; therefore walking a section of a river or being fortunate to travel from the source to mouth of a river will invite pupils to observe and respond to patterns and processes, change and development in the natural environment. Some pupils may need scaffolding activities during a nature walk of this kind to encourage them to observe more deeply. One way to instigate this is by providing pupils with a set of photographs of what they will see on the walk. As they walk along, pupils should try to match the photographs to the actual environment and place these in order. They can then share these photo journeys and talk about what they see with visual clues as support. In order to differentiate this activity, pupils could take photos as they walk. Asking pupils to look carefully and to select one special feature to photograph brings personal choice into the river walk and begins to support pupils in finding a special attachment to the place.

RIVERS THROUGH PLAY

If pupils are to think creatively about rivers, they need to have a reason to do this and engage with the experience. There are a number of games which could begin a river investigation to help motivate pupils and inspire them to want to know more about the river. Asking pupils to point to features, such as 'point to the direction of the source', may appear simple; however it will draw on pupils' observational skills, their knowledge of the river's current and their understanding of the features. If you are based at one location, bring two dice: one with the numbers 1–6 and one dice with the senses look, smell, feel and hear written on the faces (two senses would need to be written twice). Throw the senses dice and the number dice. Pupils must give examples of that sense at the river site – the number of examples is determined by the dice. This will focus and spark discussion about whether everyone hears and smells in the same way and will encourage children to stop, look and listen more deeply. Playing the 'Five Whys Game' will develop talk around rivers. Asking pupils to say something they observe and asking why is it this way will

Figure 8.2 What can we observe along a river?

promote them to give a response to which the teacher asks why again. In each 'why' question pupils delve deeper and challenge their observational and critical thinking.

RIVERS THROUGH ART

Nature as an artist works in creative ways along a river, with colours and patterns constantly changing through natural and human processes. Investigating colours and creating a palette of colours at a river site encourages pupils to look with artists' eyes. It moves away from the idea of geographical or mathematical patterns to consider nature as an artist within its natural canvas. Creating a colour wheel before arriving at the river site will help pupils to seek out colours in the environment. However to develop pupils' creative awareness, pupils can create the colour wheel at the river site. Asking questions such as 'how many shades of brown do we need?' or 'how can you create that colour on your colour wheel?' will develop pupils' artistic viewpoint of the river. At some river sites, pupils may be able to create their colour wheel using natural materials such as flowers and leaves. Pupils could work on a landscape drawing of the river completing half the drawing with natural materials and the second half with colouring pencils. In their reflection pupils can discuss which half of the picture gives a more accurate image of the river and why, thus providing an opportunity for artistic interpretation. Pickering (2015) describes using 'wordglyphs' or word art to promote creative and artistic field sketches where the words used are designed to personify the river or the action. So a fast section of the river is labelled with *fast* looking letters, for example.

RIVERS THROUGH CONCEPTS

Creativity can be generated by supporting children to think conceptually in that they begin to move away from a list of facts to generating questions and ideas relating to the holistic qualities of the river. Concepts that align with rivers could be:

■ Systems
■ Form and Function
■ Change
■ Development or Conflict
■ Responsibility
■ Interdependence
■ Space and Place.

There are a host of ways in which concepts could be used to promote creativity. One response could be to encourage pupils to select one concept which they are going to focus on at the river. Their role is to create questions and collect data which links to their concept. Alternatively, the teacher could have the concepts written on outlines of large glasses to visualise the conceptual lens approach. Erickson (2008) explains that 'the conceptual lens pulls thinking to the conceptual and transferable levels, and integrates thinking between the factual and conceptual levels' (p.105). As pupils investigate the river, the teacher holds up a conceptual lens (the glasses) and asks the class to formulate their work around this concept. The teacher may set a conceptual question to support pupils such as: 'How are rivers influenced by time, space and place?' 'Can words alone describe what you see at the river?' Concepts could be subject driven or creative pupils could be encouraged to find conceptual understanding across more than one discipline.

RIVERS THROUGH TECHNOLOGY

Digital cameras and iPads prove invaluable for capturing river activities and provide data for teacher assessment. Back in the classroom pupils can watch their film footage in slow motion, adding a narrative to what they see. Photos can become part of their reflections, being used as evidence of something that happened or was observed.

River processes are challenging in themselves and become instantly real at a river site. Pupils may want to capture this by creating their own river broadcast. Before reaching the river site, teachers can explain to the class that their role is to create a documentary. At the river site, pupils then have a focus. They use talk through dramatic techniques to explain the river processes in action whilst integrating geographical vocabulary. Pupils can dress in costume and take on different roles and edit their work back in the classroom. Alternatively pupils could share their river experience through a blog or app. This works particularly well when pupils have journeyed two sections of the river. Pupils can make a free choice of how to develop their app and, alongside the teacher, the class can write the assessment criteria to ensure there is a balance between geographical vocabulary, examples and personal reflections on the experience.

Applications based on rivers are increasing and the Environment Agency has developed a river and sea levels 'app' (see web links at end of chapter). This can be used as research into river patterns or as part of the risk assessment to note safe places to visit along the river. The Tiltmeter App can be used at the river site as another form of measuring.

Transferring understanding from 2D maps to aerial photos to actual rivers is a complex skill and one that requires pupils to understand the variations in how rivers are portrayed. Using Google Maps before, during and after the visit will go some way to developing pupils' skills. Where iPads can be taken into the field, the Skitch App allows pupils to annotate over maps and images and therefore record their thinking instantly at the location. This works well when more than one part of the river will be investigated. If your school has a drone, this could be used to record the river's flow and is another way for pupils to reflect back in the classroom.

When at the river site, pupils could create their own geocaches including data found at the site. They could leave field sketches of the site and bar graphs to show data collected. Pupils will enjoy thinking about a safe place to hide this geocache considering the factors which may affect its longevity. In this way, the class are preparing evidence for the following year's children. The next class will be able to hunt for these 'river caches' and analyse the data. What has changed? What has stayed the same? The new class can then add to the geocache and so the cycle continues.

RIVERS THROUGH PHILOSOPHY

Depending on the location of the river site, encourage the pupils to group together to conduct a Philosophy for Children (P4C) session. Pupils may feel more inspired to share thoughts and ideas when they physically see the river and draw on evidence in front of them. They are likely to feel more compassion about littering if they can see the effect it is having. They are more likely to ask 'why' questions if they have stood near to a broken flood defence. Questions which may begin discussions could be: Who owns the river? Is it right to tame Mother Nature? How sustainable is a river? What is our relationship with the river? What is beautiful about the river? Why is the river polluted? The notion of valuing beauty and seeing connections to and with nature is explored further in the work of HRH The Prince of Wales (2010). Through P4C creative pupils will begin to see the connections they have with nature and how this impacts their world in terms of their relationship and understanding of it. In some cases it may encourage pupils to take action and help to sustain the river environment. This idea is supported by Robinson (2015) who explains the essential need to develop students' 'unique capacities for creative thought and action' (p.136).

RIVERS THROUGH READING

Bringing a 'living library' to the outdoors will encourage pupils to make connections between the written word and the reality of the outdoors. In terms of bringing non-fiction texts, pupils can read about the theory of the processes and observe these in action. Is the book always correct? Is there an example of the process happening in our river? Pupils could also use non-fiction texts to support their field sketches in terms of having the key vocabulary and being able to label their work accurately. Pupils could write their own text books, or complete a documentary on camera.

Bringing the fictional world to the river allows teachers to introduce stories with a river theme. Creation stories for instance often begin along a river. As the words are read, pupils can begin to imagine the 'birth' of the river or a place along the river. They can bring these stories alive at the river site and consider why characters would have made certain decisions by role-playing situations.

RIVERS THROUGH WRITING

Lewis (2010) explains that 'another key idea is to think of a river as a system with distinctive "inputs" and "outputs"' (p.255). Connecting back to the idea of concepts, pupils can be asked to think like the river. Just as they have systems and routines in school, so does the river. Why does the river flow that way? Why does the river deposit materials? Why might the river flood here? Why is the bridge built here? What materials are used for the flood defences and why? This could be developed into persuasive writing, where pupils personify the river and advertise their creative design capabilities, including drawings and diagrams to explain their techniques. In terms of fiction, pupils could write poems in which they become the river. In this way pupils begin to think about the systems of rivers and portray these in an artistic way. Back in the classroom, pupils could read their poems accompanying them to music they select. A further way to develop this idea could be to place a piece of cauliflower or broccoli in the river. Pupils can predict what they think the river will do with the vegetable. If pupils film the event they can then describe and explain what the river does through their poetry.

RIVERS THROUGH MATHS

A creative thinker is one who takes time to reflect, to step back from a learning situation and consider ways to develop, strengthen or completely change their ideas and one way to promote this could be through a river investigation leading to a river report. In setting this up as an enquiry cycle, those pupils who require support can be guided through the experience. The river investigation suggested below emphasises the relationship between Interrogatory and Exploratory talk (Alexander, 2008, p.38), creative and critical thinking, use of secondary sources and reflection and evaluation – all of which stem from the definition of creativity set out by Desailly (2015).

In an article in the *Primary Geographer* journal, Bound (2010) summarises effective outdoor learning experiences as those that allow pupils 'the freedom and time to explore their surroundings and put theories into a context they will understand and be able to access in the future' (p.31). The purpose of a river investigation leading into a report gives pupils the chance to do just this and to test theories about a river through meaningful data collection.

Taking an enquiry approach, the teacher begins by introducing the river site location through digital maps or OS Maps. This would ideally take place at the mid-point of a unit when pupils are familiar with river features and some of the main processes. Teachers then challenge pupils to consider ways they could creatively find out more about the river using the resources in the classroom or materials from home. Pupils may also decide to use secondary sources to enquire into how others would approach the task and develop their own ideas from these. Pupils should be encouraged to make use of skills across the curriculum to aid their enquiry. The following example of a report comes from work with a year 5/6 class but could be adapted for younger age pupils.

- Creating a field sketch: this encourages pupils to observe features and aims to apply their knowledge by labelling the sketch accurately.
- Measuring velocity: within the river report, pupils can reflect on the process they used to measure the river's speed.

Measuring the depth...

how?

To measure the depth of the river I used a metre stick in 3 spots. Initially they should have been 4 spots but then, because we could not go to the other side of the river, they became 3 spots.

Results:

SPOT:	Results:
in the middle	36 cm
on the right	60 cm
on the left	33 cm

Average=
$$\frac{36+60+33}{3} = 43 cm$$

Diagram:

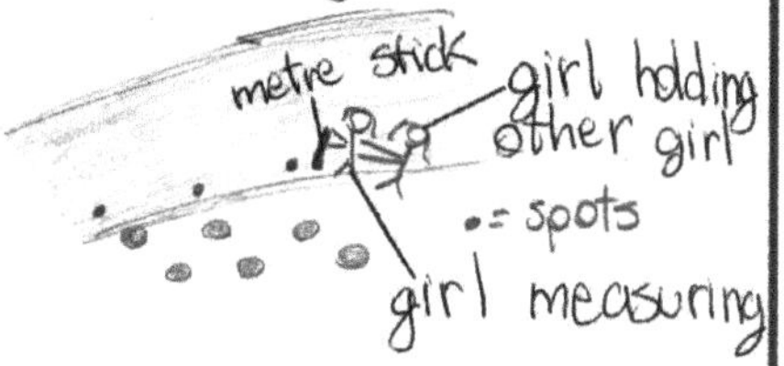

metre stick girl holding other girl

.= spots

girl measuring

The Results were not so precise because we could not go very far from the bank and maybe the metre stick was not straight in the river. This can affect the accuracy of the results because

Figure 8.3 A bit of maths to help solve a problem

- Measuring depth: the notion of a fair test and taking an average can be explored through this activity.
- Measuring width: if the river site is too deep or you only have access to one side of the river bank, pupils will have to think more creatively about how to measure the width.
- Pollution at the river: investigating this issue connects to work in Science through the use of pH indicator strips. In using these, pupils can compare the result of the strip to what they see around the river in terms of litter.
- Evidence of attrition: collecting rock samples to determine the levels of attrition at the river site is a wonderful way for pupils to use mathematics to show their data. Pupils can also take a creative approach by designing their own scale of roundness or they may decide to find an already produced one.
- Evidence of erosion: through observation, photographs and sketches, pupils are developing skills and looking for evidence. In the data they collect, teachers can assess the understanding pupils have about processes and their misconceptions.
- A written reflection on the fieldwork: a report of this kind will most likely create further questions and inspire pupils to return to the river site and develop their measuring techniques. Therefore asking pupils to reflect at the end of the report draws their understanding together and encourages reflection on how mathematics can help to understand more about a river.

RIVERS THROUGH SCIENCE

As pupils explore a river, they will come across a range of habitats to be investigated and observed respectfully. Taking quadrants, pooters, sampling tools, microscopes and nets for instance, pupils will be able to select from a range of tools to further their investigation and move with nature to explore it more fully. Taking a scientific view of the river, pupils can begin to understand the river's relationship to habitats. Pupils can explore why habitats have developed in certain places along the river and possible threats to these habitats. They can plan and carry out fair tests to answer their science enquiries. Pupils can study habitats over time and note changes to wildlife through photographs and written field notes, developing vocabulary to name features found. In carrying out these explorations pupils can explore the overlap between geographical and scientific processes and how mathematics can be used as a means of explaining data collected. If more than one river location can be accessed pupils can compare and contrast habitats discovered and reasons for these similarities and/or differences.

RIVERS THROUGH TIME

A creative outdoor learner will be able to appreciate that rivers have changed over time and place and that, due to a number of physical and human processes, rivers are not static. This is a challenging concept for young pupils to interpret in that where they are standing may have once been the river, for example. To support children's discoveries, the local library may have a collection of maps or photographs which show the previous river sites and therefore pupils have a visual understanding of this concept. There may also be evidence in the local area of old bridges, for example, that once transported people across the river.

A local museum may show how the river was used in the past and pupils could role play some of these activities to help their investigations.

RIVERS THROUGH DESIGN

Conducting an enquiry through a design cycle will encourage pupils to think about materials and the actions of the river. Challenging pupils to create rafts that may carry a specified object or weight will encourage trial and error. Pupils will learn that creative explorations take time, reflection and action and they will begin to understand which materials are sustainable for a design of this sort.

RIVERS THROUGH MUSIC

There are a wealth of music clips on the Internet which could be used to interpret river features such as waterfalls or meanders. Using these in a class discussion and asking pupils to predict which feature is represented will bring about talk and encourage the use of subject vocabulary. At the river site, pupils could create their own musical interpretations of the river. If pupils are able to investigate with a box of tuned and un-tuned percussion they can begin to evaluate which instruments best represent the sounds they hear at the river, thus helping pupils to appreciate the holistic view of outdoor learning. As Louv (2005) states, 'children need nature for the healthy development of their senses, and, therefore, for learning and creativity' (p.55).

RISK ASSESSMENT

Taking children to a river site has many risks and will require a high pupil to adult ratio. Robertson (2014) explains the need to shift from risk assessment to a risk-benefit assessment which is 'an approach to risk management which considers the benefits of any activity alongside the risk' (p.25). In taking this approach, teachers will find that the benefits to learning far outweigh the risks when managed effectively. In order to limit the risks to children, it is important to share photographs of the river site before a visit. Ask children to point out what could put them at risk and how the risks could be limited. Another way to ensure children are prepared for a visit is to recreate the river site from classroom objects where children can rehearse safe behaviour in advance of the visit and therefore when they arrive at the site they will feel more confident.

Any risk-benefit analysis should include a walk of the area by teachers prior to the visit. If there are pockets of rubbish or slippery banks, these can be marked on a small-scale map and shared with the children as part of the risk-benefit assessment discussions. Children need to learn how to be independent in nature and therefore by taking the initiative and considering how to manage risks they are more likely to feel part of the nature they are exploring.

CONCLUSION

The scope for fostering children's curiosity about rivers and developing this into creative explorations is endless and because rivers are never static, there is much potential to return to a river site with a different subject focus. An entire year of work could be carried out at the river site and compiled into a rivers workbook which shares the pupils' cross-curricular curious explorations. When reflecting on the notion of creativity, rivers are in themselves creative forces of nature and as teachers we are inspiring our pupils to be creative forces in the indoor and outdoor classroom. We aim for our pupils to become life-long learners and explorers and working at a river site in creative ways allows pupils to take a step towards this goal. Desailly (2015, p.58) gives a range of skills that a creative child will need to possess. Through carrying out learning at a river site, pupils have the opportunity to address many of these skills: in particular noticing, generating ideas, thinking in different spheres and being absorbed. They will embark on a journey of creative, reflective and critical thinking through a real context which they could apply to different situations in the future.

REFERENCES

Alexander, R. (2008) *Towards Dialogic Teaching. Rethinking Classroom Talk.* 4th Edn. UK: Dialogos.

Bound, S. (2010) Get out of the classroom and into a river. *Primary Geographer*, 73. Sheffield: Geographical Association.

Desailly, J. (2015) *Creativity in the Primary Classroom.* 2nd Edn. London: SAGE Publications Ltd.

Erickson, H.L. (2008) *Stirring the Head, Heart and Soul.* 3rd Edn. California: Corwin Press.

HRH The Prince of Wales (2010) *Harmony. A New Way of Looking at our World.* Great Britain: Harper Collins Publishers.

Lewis, L. (2010) *Rivers, Coasts and the Landscape.* In. S. Scoffham (ed.) *Primary Geography Handbook.* Sheffield: Geographical Association.

Louv, R. (2005) *Last Child in the Woods.* New York: Algonquin Books.

Pickering, S. (2015) Starter. *Primary Geography,* 83. Sheffield, Geographical Association.

Robertson, J. (2014) *A Beginner's Guide to Learning Outdoors.* Wales: Crown House Publishing Ltd.

Robinson, K. (2015) *Creative Schools. Revolutionizing Education from the Ground Up.* UK: Allen Lane.

Taylor. C. (2012) *Advanced Outdoor Learning. Creating a Whole-School Culture.* Somerset: Attitude Matters Publications.

FURTHER READING

Bakashaba, C. (2014) The River Nile up close. *Primary Geography,* 85. Sheffield: Geographical Association.

Burns, M. and Griffith, A. (2012) *Outstanding Teaching. Engaging Learners.* Carmarthen: Crown House Publishing.

Collis, S. (2014) Refreshing rivers. *Primary Geography*, 83. Sheffield: Geographical Association.

Jackson, K. (2015) *A Practical Guide. Outdoor Learning.* Woodbridge: National Education Trust.

King, C. (2011) Extreme earth science. *Primary Geography*, 76. Sheffield: Geographical Association.

Tanner, J. and Whittle J. (2015) *The Everyday Guide to Primary Geography. Local Fieldwork.* Sheffield: Geographical Association.

Whitburn, N. (2008) Go with the flow. *Primary Geography,* 65. Sheffield: Geographical Association.

Useful websites

Amazon: The Secrets of the Golden River (4 part series): www.youtube.com/watch?v=ZzX9de4m9EU

Clips of waterfalls: www.youtube.com/watch?v=PTgil3lympU

Develop your knowledge at: www.geography-fieldwork.org/rivers.aspx

Downloadable activity sheets: www.3dgeography.co.uk/#!river-worksheets/c18cy

Downloadable resources: https://canalrivertrust.org.uk/explorers/teachers

Facts and Images to use in the classroom: www.channel4learning.com/sites/essentials/geography/units/rivers_bi.shtml

Fieldwork techniques: www.connectedonline.co.uk/ProtectedMaterial/VirtualTours/river_esk/Fieldwork_techniques.pdf

Rivers class clips: www.bbc.co.uk/education/topics/zqdwxnb/resources/1

River features: meanders and oxbow lakes: www.youtube.com/watch?v=4qKS_Nk7UmY

River habitats: www.wildlifewatch.org.uk/explore-wildlife/habitats/freshwater-and-wet-places

River and sea levels app: http://apps.environment-agency.gov.uk/river-and-sea-levels/default.aspx

River techniques: www.rgs.org/OurWork/Schools/Fieldwork+and+local+learning/Fieldwork+techniques/Rivers.htm

Support for teachers: www.lotc.org.uk/

Sustainable water resources: www.thewaterpage.com/

Tools and Resources to use at the river: http://riversandpeople.com/school-resources/

Why do rivers curve: www.youtube.com/watch?v=8a3r-cG8Wic

2 Minute Geology: What is a meander: www.youtube.com/watch?v=STgbHFvUMlE

Books for the reading corner

Bowden, R. (2005) *Rivers Through Time. Settlements of the River Thames.* Oxford: Heinemann Library. (A series of books.)

Evans, M. (2015) *The Pooh Sticks Handbook.* London: Egmont UK Ltd.

Gallagher, D. (2008) *River and Sea Homes.* London: Macmillan.

Ganeri, A. (2014) *Exploring Rivers: A Benjamin Blog and His Inquisitive Dog Investigation.* London: Raintree.

Gardiner, B. (2014) *Rivers, Erosion & Flooding Active Learning Pack.* Southampton: Oaka Books.

Green, J. (2009) *The Rhine: Journey Along the River.* London: Wayland.

Green, J. (2011) *Rivers Around the World.* London: Wayland.

Leake, D. (2014) *Rivers and Streams.* London: Raintree.

Llewellyn, C. (2001) *Using the River.* Essex: Harcourt Education Ltd.

Manning, P. (2014) *Thames (River Adventures).* London: Franklin Watts. (A series of books.)

Miles, L. (2003) *Water and Rivers.* Oxford: Oxford University Press.

Sweeney, A. (2011) *Rivers.* Minnesota: Capstone Press.

Taylor, B. (2006) *River and Inland Water Habitats.* New York: Gareth Stevens Publishing.

Thomson, R. (2013) *Geography Corner: Rivers.* London: Wayland.

Throp, C. (2012) *The River Nile.* London: Raintree.

Waldon, M. (2013) *Rivers.* London: Raintree.

Wilkins, J. (2014) *What can Live in a River?* London: Raintree.

CHAPTER 9

CREATIVE APPROACHES FOR TEACHING PHYSICAL EDUCATION IN THE OUTDOORS

Sarah Williams

INTRODUCTION

This chapter discusses the relationship between physical education and outdoor learning. It focuses on a range of aspects of outdoor learning including adventurous activity and the development of outdoor learning experiences on both school sites and with residential trips. The chapter considers the benefits of outdoor and adventurous activities on children's social and emotional development.

DEFINING OUTDOOR EDUCATION WITHIN PHYSICAL EDUCATION

Outdoor education has been a discrete programme of study within primary school physical education (PE) programmes for several years. On the whole outdoor education within PE has, however, been limited to the curriculum for upper Key Stage 2 pupils with very little exposure to outdoor learning for Key Stage 1 children. PE has been part of the national curriculum since the early 1940s and was formally established as a key programme of study in the Education Reform Act in 1988. Since this time PE has evolved from a physical drill based regime to a more varied programme of study, developing learners' physical skills along with a knowledge and understanding of health and fitness, games, aquatics and creative disciplines such as dance. In fairly recent times Outdoor and Adventurous Activity (OAA) has become a discrete part of most primary schools' PE programme. Since its inclusion it has evolved and become widely acknowledged as a fundamental activity to support the development of children's personal and social skills.

Learning Outside the Classroom, Outdoor Education and Outdoor and Adventurous Activity are terms commonly used by teachers when describing outdoor activity within physical education. It is important to recognise these terms because whilst they may be referring to similar activity and could be used by some professionals interchangeably, they may also be to referring to different approaches to learning in primary schools.

Learning Outside the Classroom (LOtC) is specifically focused on providing experiences outside and beyond the typical outdoor PE spaces and, more often than not, will not specifically include objectives related to physical education. It is focused on providing children with exciting opportunities to explore an environment and could include the wider school grounds or local community spaces such as woods and parklands. Activities could include orienteering type tasks but the focus will not predominantly be on the development of the physical aspects of this activity. It is likely that most LOtC will be cross-curricular and it could be a term used to describe learning in the outdoors that does not include physical activity at all.

> Learning outside the classroom should be built into planning for *all* learners, *every* week and *all* year round. It is a powerful tool that is proven to raise attainment, bolster social, emotional and personal development and contributes to the health and well-being of children and young people.
>
> (LOtC 2011)

Outdoor Education (OE) is usually concerned with the activity of moving and learning in the outdoors but also concerned with engaging with the environment. This term is likely to be relevant when describing residential and adventure-based experiences that often go beyond the typical programme of activities designed within PE. Activities are designed to promote self-reliance and are positioned in environments that provide challenge beyond the typical school surroundings. These activities are selected for their ability to reveal opportunities for learners to develop positive relationships and challenge perceptions of self. It seeks to use the outdoors to foster positive relationships, cooperation and collaboration, developing respect for self, peers and the natural environment. Activities often selected to foster these experiences and skills may include trust-based games, water-based pursuits and high ropes courses. Most OE practitioners would agree as a concept that OE includes:

▨ an educational element which stimulates personal and social development;
▨ an experience which will usually include adventure and challenge;
▨ learning as an experiential process which utilises direct experience;
▨ an increased self and social awareness plus increased awareness of community and environment.

Outdoor activities within physical education are often named *Outdoor and Adventurous Activities (OAA)*. This is a broad term that includes activities that enable young people to learn how to respond positively to challenge and responsibility, to manage risk, cope with adversity and work positively with others. This activity could be based on a school site, local outdoor space or at a residential centre. The teaching of this key aspect of learning within the PE national curriculum should essentially be a practical, physical and, where safely possible, child led enquiry based activity.

Types of activities often included in schools' outdoor and adventurous programmes:

▨ Problem solving activities
▨ Cooperative activities

■ Trust activities
■ Orienteering activities
■ Communication activities.

These activities are not likely to be areas of activity that take place every week in most schools but they shouldn't be exclusive to Key Stage 2 learners. All children can benefit from these activities and in most instances they can be designed to be fully inclusive. Due to the nature of many of these activities they are also valuable in a programme of activities supporting the development of language.

OUTDOOR LEARNING ON YOUR SCHOOL SITE

ACTIVITY BOX **PROBLEM SOLVING ACTIVITY IN ACTION**

Magic cane

Task: Teams of 4–6 members are given a magic cane that they must lower to the ground, using just their index fingers. All participants must remain in contact with it at all times.

Equipment: 1 thin bamboo cane for each group (*make sure the edges are flush*).

Space: inside or out.

Activity:
■ Split the class into small groups of 4–6 and have team members facing each other (2 facing 2 or 3 facing 3).
■ Hand each group a cane.
■ Ask all of the children to hold their arms out in front of them, pointing their index fingers out.
■ Place the cane across the fingers of each group and get the group to hold the cane horizontal until you tell them to start.
■ Every team member must have 2 index fingers in contact with the cane.
■ Explain that the challenge is to lower the cane to the ground ensuring everyone's index fingers are in contact with the cane at all times. Pinching, hooking or grabbing is not permitted – it must rest on top of fingers only.
■ Reiterate to the group that if anyone's finger is caught not touching the cane, the challenge will be restarted.

As an extension activity you could run this activity blindfolded.

■ **Figure 9.1** The magic cane!

ACTIVITY BOX **COOPERATIVE ACTIVITIES IN ACTION**

Magic carpet

Equipment: 5 large pieces of carpet or fabric or thin gymnastics mats.

Space: indoor or outdoor.

Activity: The idea is that the children have found a magic carpet and they have been flying around the world exploring magical lands, meeting wonderful people. They have arrived back at home but have found that they cannot land because the carpet is upside down!

■ Stand each team of 6 children on a mat that is big enough to hold the whole team whilst still leaving 1/3 exposed.
■ Without anyone getting off the mat, the team must flip the carpet over.
■ The first team to do this wins but if anyone touches the floor the task must be started again.
■ Successful teams will flip one opposite corner, bow-tie style and gradually shift players on to the right side of the mat.

ACTIVITY BOX **TRUST ACTIVITIES IN ACTION**

Human chair

Equipment: no equipment needed.

Space: inside or out but with KS1 best placed on a soft grassy area.

Activity:
■ Ask your class to form 2 circles (approximately 15 in each circle).
■ Get the children to turn one shoulder out of the circle and one in, ensuring they are all facing the same direction.
■ Get the group to work together to keep shape as they gently shuffle sideways forming a tight circle.
■ On your command the children will gently sit back on to the knee of the person behind them.

As an extension activity get the group to sit, then stand and remove one person from the circle at a time to see how few people can be in a group without falling.

■ **Figure 9.2** The human chair!

ACTIVITY BOX **ORIENTEERING ACTIVITIES IN ACTION**

Circle of friends

Equipment: paper and marker pens.

Space: hall, yard or large classroom space.

Activity:

- Sit your children in a circle formation and include yourself.
- Leave room between the children for someone to walk.
- Draw a 'map' of the circle of children (identify children with a circle) and draw a symbol to represent you in the circle.
- Proceed to add the names of a couple of children. As you do this point to a circle and ask the class to name who is sat in that position.
- Now turn the map upside down and ask children for a few more names by the same method (they usually twist their head to match the view of the map) until all names are included.
- Now get the class to help to identify a simple route on the map you have created, e.g. across the circle, around the person opposite and back to their starting place.
- Draw some other routes for different children to follow and gradually make them more complicated (use different coloured markers for different routes).

Once your class has been through this process you can get them to design their own circle of friends map. You can gradually make the space bigger, replace the children with cones with symbols on them or use landmarks in your playground.

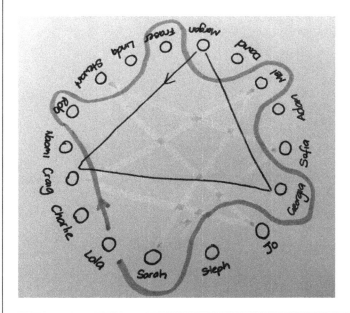

■ **Figure 9.3**
A circle of friends

ACTIVITY BOX **COMMUNICATION ACTIVITIES IN ACTION**

Blind square

Equipment: 4 long ropes and blindfolds for all of the class.

Space: inside or out but with KS1 best placed on a soft grassy area.

Activity: To form a perfect square using the one rope. Tie the rope in a square for KS1 but leave untied for KS2.

- ■ Divide the class up into groups of 6–8.
- ■ Hand all but one person in each group a blindfold. Give the un-blindfolded member the rope to place into both hands of the blindfolded team members. *Make sure the shape they form with the rope is not square from the start.*
- ■ The one un-blindfolded team member is the main communicator. Only the communicator can talk, the other team members must not let go of the rope or take off blindfolds.
- ■ The communicator cannot touch the team members but must offer instruction to guide the group to form a square with the rope.

This activity can be repeated several times but start with your strongest communicator. You may find you need to support KS1 children at first or put them in pairs.

■ **Figure 9.4**
Blind square

BEYOND THE PHYSICAL

Educators are acutely aware of the role they play in developing and maintaining a positive, safe and purposeful learning environment. Most schools have policies and programmes in place promoting a positive learning environment and a culture of trust and personal challenge. Emotional health and wellbeing is of course not a new concept for schools; however, more than ever before, we are seeing a more intense focus on the development of activities to enable learners to develop characteristics such as resilience and determination. In recent years we have seen schools focus on a number of models and approaches to support the social and emotional development of learners. Many of these will probably be familiar to you including the practice of mindfulness, an understanding of emotional intelligence and the development of growth mindsets. Outdoor and Adventurous Activity can contribute to the facilitation of many of these models and approaches.

Daniel Goleman (1996) identified the following personal characteristics of 'emotional intelligence' that determine how we manage ourselves:

- Self-awareness: self-confidence and sense of one's self-worth and capabilities.
- Self-regulation: trustworthiness, responsibility and the ability to adapt to change.
- Motivation: commitment to achieve a goal, persistence and striving to do one's best.
- Empathy: understanding others, providing support and encouragement.
- Social skills: negotiation, working with others to achieve a shared goal, inspiring and leading others.

If you reflect back to the start of this chapter where we define Outdoor Education and Outdoor and Adventurous Activities, can you see a link between the characteristics identified by Daniel Goleman and the characteristics fostered through the effective teaching of Outdoor Education? Table 9.1 explores these relationships.

Table 9.1 Exploring the relationships between the characteristics of effective creative teaching activities outdoors

Characteristics of emotional intelligence	Characteristics fostered through OE	Example
Self-awareness	Trust based activities that challenge children's emotions	Human chair and other tasks that develop confidence in self and the team
Self-regulation	Communication and problem solving tasks that require children to negotiate and work effectively as a team	Blind square and other tasks that require children to act responsibly and consider others' needs
Motivation	Problem solving tasks that require effective team work to succeed	Magic cane and activities that require perseverance and determination
Empathy	Cooperative and trust activities that rely on effective team work and consideration of individuals' strengths and challenges	Magic carpet and tasks that require teams to work methodically through challenges ensuring everyone is involved
Social skills	Cooperative and communication tasks that involve negotiation and listening skills	Circle of friends and other orienteering based activities that require effective communication skills and negotiation

EMOTIONAL INTELLIGENCE IN ACTION THROUGH PE

Parachute games

Parachute games are popular activities that encourage learners to work co-operatively, share a common goal and demonstrate self-regulation. Parachute activities are easily managed as they can include a whole class of children and are always met with high levels of enthusiasm. Open-ended and high-order questioning could focus on a range of learning outcomes including social and cooperative aspects of learning.

ACTIVITY BOX **MUSHROOM**

- ▨ Spread your class of children evenly around the parachute to form a circle, while holding the edge.
- ▨ Pull the parachute taut and then ask the children to lower it to their knee height.
- ▨ On your signal, all the children raise the parachute upwards so it will fill with air and rise up like a giant mushroom.

Get children to practise this action together so they appreciate the need for cooperation and working together as a group.

Ask the children what they could try as a group to get it as high as possible. If the group work together and all take a couple steps towards the centre as the chute rises, will it make a taller mushroom?

Developing the mushroom task

Once the basic action of mushroom play is successful, experiment with different ideas produced from your discussion with the class.

How could we . . .?
What might happen if . . .?
Why do you think . . .?

- ▨ You could call 'Mushroom' and get all children to run towards the centre while still holding the parachute.
- ▨ You could call 'Mushroom' and then ask all children to let go of the chute at exactly the same time (*if there isn't any wind, the chute will retain its perfect puff shape and rise straight up into the air*).
- ▨ You could experiment in an indoor and outdoor space.

Thunderstorm

Once again ask all of the children to spread out evenly around the parachute. Ask the class to then crouch down holding the parachute close to the floor.
Ask the class:

- ▨ What could we do to create a gentle breeze for the parachute?
- ▨ How could the breeze move across or along the parachute?
- ▨ Ask the children if they can feel a change in the air . . . what do we think might be following the wind? Get the children to pretend that it has started to rain. As it rains have the children stand and gently tap feet on the floor to make the sounds of the rain pattering on the floor.

■ Ask the children if they think the rain is getting heavier. Ask the class to speed up their foot tapping and then you make a loud stomping sound. Ask 'What might that have been? Oh no, the rain has turned into a thunderstorm!'

■ Ask the children to recreate the storm with quicker movements to simulate the storm.

Roller ball

This activity calls on good cooperative skills.

■ Ask all of the children to spread out evenly around the parachute and gently pull back on it to make it taut.

■ Explain what is about to happen to the class and ask them what we need to do as a class to be successful. The object of this game is to try to make the ball roll all the way around the edge of the parachute.

■ Place a large ball in front of you near the edge of the parachute and start it rolling.

■ As it comes towards each child they need to lower the parachute slightly and then as it passes they need to raise the parachute back to the original height. This takes considerable control!

■ When the whole class does this action smoothly a wave is created that pushes the ball in a steady circle.

■ Once your class has this mastered you can then play this game at different heights, change the direction the ball rolls or even clap your hands for a sudden change of direction.

Learning occurs during these types of activities when you allow experimentation and ask questions that encourage children to develop a greater appreciation of the complexity of these tasks. Model the types of behaviour you want to see and reward learners who are exhibiting positive social and emotional learning skills.

SAFETY

Outdoor learning should facilitate enjoyment of the outdoors and enable adventure. When teaching in the outdoors it is important that we maintain perspective in terms of risk and challenge to ensure that children's learning isn't stifled by the educator's risk aversion. It is widely acknowledged that children need to learn about risk. The Royal Society for the Prevention of Accidents (RoSPA) argues that children need challenges: 'It is essential to their healthy growth and development. Children need to learn about risk, about their own capabilities and to develop the mechanism for judging it in controlled settings' (Cook and Heseltine 1999, p.4). I think the hardest part of facilitating adventurous activities for teachers is learning to step back and allow children to engage in 'trial and error' activities and to resolve problems and conflict. We know through playground buddy programmes that with the right support, children can effectively manage their emotions and negotiate risk effectively. Indeed Forest School ideology focuses on children developing through activities that they initiate and explore. There is a strong child-led focus that many children learn within early years settings where they are encouraged to problem solve on both an academic level and also with social interaction. Children learn to manage mistakes; even to view getting things wrong as an important part of learning. The role of adventurous and PE based activities for later years children can help to strengthen the learning from Forest School and some play based philosophies from their early years, providing a firmer foundation for developing independence and motivation to succeed.

It is important that the following skills are built into our outdoor learning activities:

▒ Learners can identify the potential dangers associated with an outdoor activity.
▒ Learners can identify ways to ensure both their own safety and that of others when participating in an outdoor activity.
▒ Learners can use safe practices and basic risk management strategies when participating in an outdoor activity.

GUIDING RISK MANAGEMENT STRATEGIES

One of the most important strategies you can undertake to minimise risk is to involve learners in risk assessment and planning. This may be facilitated in a school hall prior to a gymnastics lesson or in a new outdoor learning environment. Do you know of any activities that can be used to introduce this idea to the children?

Steps you can take to raise awareness and encourage children to take responsibility for managing risk and personal safety:

▒ Ensure all children are concentrating as you provide an overview for the lesson and set out explicit expectations.
▒ Walk the children around the space and ask them to raise concerns relating to the safety and potential risks.
▒ Ask children what it means to work effectively and responsibly as a team and ask how they can demonstrate these skills.
▒ If the children are lifting and moving pieces of equipment, model safe techniques.
▒ When using blindfolds ensure children understand that they are responsible for ensuring their partner is safe, that they keep an eye on their partner at all times and check the space is clear of tripping hazards.
▒ Ask children to consider the conditions and activities and assess if they dressed appropriately.
▒ With the children check the equipment is safe, in good repair and being used for the purpose it is intended.

BUILDING RISK MANAGEMENT INTO YOUR ACTIVITIES

To develop children's understanding of their role in supporting each other through practical trust based activities, look to begin with low-level challenges that encourage children to make decisions. Before the children begin this activity, explain it to them and ask the group to compile a list of the risks that this activity may present. Develop a safety plan with the children identifying a few basic rules such as an agreed maximum lifting height.

ACTIVITY BOX **ALL ABOARD**

To prepare your children for activity where they will need to work effectively together and in close physical proximity, start with some simple challenges such as All Aboard to establish boundaries and promote trust:

■   Organise the children into teams of 8–10.

■   Mark out a square 60 cm by 60 cm on a grass area, using rope, string, or skipping ropes.

■   Ask each team to organise themselves within this square, ensuring no part of anyone's body touches the ground outside the square.

■   Once a position has been achieved, the team is to hold this position for 30 seconds.

After an initial attempt, give each child an opportunity to express how well the team worked together, how safe they felt and to discuss how they can help to make people feel comfortable when working in close contact with others.

RISK MANAGEMENT – OFFSITE ACTIVITY

Guiding your children through the process for managing risk through an offsite orienteering activity

Before you leave school:

■   Locate the venue where you will base your orienteering route with your class. Ask the children to use Google maps or Google Earth to develop an awareness of the surrounding area prior to your visit. Don't you need to actually walk round the course? Can the children use Google Earth prior to the orienteering activity as a lesson to merge geography and PE?

■   Plan the trip:
  - Take a look at the weather forecast for the day – do we need any specific clothing?
  - How long will it take us to walk to the park and will we be crossing any main roads? Do you think we need additional adult support to ensure the class can travel safely and navigate roads? What else might we consider to make sure we are safe and visible when walking to the park?

■   Research the park:
  - What facilities are available?
  - Can we find shelter if needed?
  - What kind of environment is it? Do we need specific footwear? See if anyone has been there before, they might be able to help to answer your questions.
  - What do you think you will see at the park? Make a list or draw a picture.

Think about safety and possible risks. If you can see a possible risk or danger, can you think of a way to make it safe? See Tables 9.2 and 9.3 for examples.

Table 9.2 Risk for the class

Risk/danger	Keeping safe
Getting lost in the park	Stay with my group Make sure we can see/hear the teacher at all times
Getting cold and wet	Take warm, waterproof clothing
Falling and tripping	Watch where you step, wear appropriate footwear and make sure your group act sensibly

Table 9.3 Risk for the environment

Risk/danger	Keeping safe
Disturbing the wildlife	Walk along quietly and carefully
Dropping litter	Put wrappers in my pocket, pick up litter
Damage to trees and plants	Keep to paths and leave plants alone

You could collate group risk assessments and ask a class to create a code of safety and code of conduct for the class. You should probably give the county council risk assessment spiel here – formal risk assessment.

As you discuss the groups' risk assessments identify any other risks that the class may not have identified and ensure they understand the reasons why these risks are relevant.

When you arrive at the site for your activity, walk the children around the area so they can make connections between what they saw during their class based research and the actual environment. Ask the children to review the risk assessments they developed and consider if anything else needs to be added. This process will help to re-establish safe practice with the children prior to the start of the practical activity.

Local authorities, academy chains and schools will have policies related to the safe management of risk and outdoor learning. Teachers and leaders of activities need to be aware of the school's policies and procedures and the formal process for carrying out risk assessments. If you are in any doubt ensure you seek guidance and support from senior leaders. School policy related to safe management of activity and managing risk will be guided by governors and will be reviewed in an annual cycle of policy review. Guidance is constantly evolving so ensure you regularly review policies when planning activity.

When planning for activity led by external partners or based at a residential site, schools need to be familiar with the risk assessments that have been developed by the providers of activity and check they adequately meet the needs of your specific children and your school's health and safety guidance.

Further information and guidance in relation to health and safety can be found at: www.hse.gov.uk/services/education/school-trips.pdf.

An activity is judged to be safe in physical education where the risks associated with the activity are deemed to be acceptably low. It is the responsibility of all those who teach physical education to identify those risks and decide whether the level of risk is acceptable. They should do this through good teaching and management of a situation on a day-to-day basis and a good awareness of the school policies. Much outdoor learning takes place with very low levels of risk but, on occasion, risk may be at a more significant level. It is desirable to balance risks and benefits in any experience to ensure that actions are proportionate and reasonable. There is a legal requirement for a process of risk assessment to take place in many outdoor learning contexts. This is important, but do not lose sight of the benefits to be had from the experience and the need to balance these against the risks.

CONCLUSION

It is clear that physical education lessons often take place outdoors. Indeed throughout much of late Spring and Summer children can look forward to PE lessons outside. Weather does not have to be a barrier to taking PE outside. Yes, we have to be mindful of the hazards of running on wet, slippy surfaces, but there are many activities that help children develop coordination, teamwork and problem-solving skills, and develop resilience through managing success and failure, that can take place both inside and outside. PE is a versatile subject area which can contribute much to children's holistic development and it is hoped that through the PE lessons of their primary years children feel motivated and skilled to continue with healthy exercise and respect for their natural environment throughout their lives.

REFERENCES

Goleman, D. (1996) *Emotional Intelligence*. London, Bloomsbury.

Cook, B. and Heseltine, P. (1999) *Assessing Risk on Children's Playgrounds* (2nd edn). Birmingham, RoSPA.

LOtC (2011) *What is LOtC?* Available at: www.lotc.org.uk/what-is-lotc/ (accessed November 2016).

CHAPTER 10

CREATIVE APPROACHES TO TEACHING THROUGH ADVENTURE

Lee Pritchard and Colin Wood

INTRODUCTION

> Britain has a long tradition of involving young people in adventurous outdoor
> activities, and the positive impact this can have on a young person's education is
> widely acknowledged.
>
> (Outdoor Education Advisers' Panel 2015: 1)

This chapter explores the more adventurous side of teaching outdoors, and why this is a powerful approach to primary school teaching. It examines ways to engage with outdoor activities, how to incorporate them into primary teaching and how to create adventures on or off the school grounds. Using case studies of orienteering and rock-climbing, the chapter shows how teaching through adventure can provide primary children with opportunities to explore real and imaginary environments, to face personal and shared challenges, and through that to develop an understanding of their own abilities and a respect for their environment and for other people. This chapter looks at preparation and planning, running adventures and reflecting on them afterwards. There are helpful tips on encouraging creativity and useful creative tasks that encourage children to use their imaginations and work together. The chapter also provides advice and examples on how schools can access support and training in order to deliver adventurous activities.

This chapter is mainly written for people working in primary schools but we hope will be of interest to others. It responds to concerns about the sedentary lifestyles of young people and the limited opportunities for children to learn about appropriate risk-taking. Whilst the arguments about child safety and overprotection are a focus of much discussion we have opted to leave this to the reader and instead have developed pragmatic advice for teaching through adventure. If readers wish to explore the evidence they could look at Pether (2012), who shows that learning outside the classroom can have a positive impact on pupil engagement, achievement, progress, attainment and attendance, and thus that it supports the school improvement agenda.

■ **Figure 10.1** Children enjoying the Welsh mountains

WHAT IS OUTDOOR ADVENTURE?

So what are the essential elements of an outdoor adventure? Swarbrooke et al. (2003: 9) list the core characteristics of adventure as: uncertain outcomes, danger and risk, challenge, anticipated rewards, novelty, stimulation and excitement, escapism and separatism, exploration and discovery, absorption and focus, and contrasting emotions.

This list probably sounds a little scary to the adult reader and seems a long way from the normal practice of primary teaching. However if we were able to slip into the mind of a primary age child we would probably find that their most enjoyable and memorable experiences fit well with these characteristics. Indeed in her study of adult memories of childhood, Waite (2007) found that 135 out of 241 responses linked specific positive memories of childhood with adventure, risk and challenge. So it is possible to see that adventure is both a memorable part of childhood and a source of enjoyment.

As outdoor experiences are memorable and enjoyable they provide opportunities for teachers to use outdoor adventure as a medium for delivering aspects of the curriculum. Indeed there is a long history of primary schools using outdoor adventure as a medium for teaching either as an extension of classroom learning, or to develop confidence and a sense of self. In an age when many primary aged children spend long periods of time involved in virtual adventures through their electronic devices, outdoor adventure provides a link to the physical reality of the world outside – a reality that does not include a reset button. These outdoor adventures encourage children to learn to cope with the real world and to develop confidence in their own abilities as well as encouraging them to work with others. Gill (2010) recommends that the educators' focus should not simply be on delivering a curriculum, but on providing children with the opportunities to develop confidence, resilience and a sense of responsibility, not forgetting the importance of enjoyment, excitement and engagement with the world outside of the confines of the classroom.

TEACHING THROUGH ADVENTURE: WHAT IT IS NOT . . .

Before looking at teaching through adventure, we would like to explore what it is not.

Teaching through adventure is not about play

Play is an essential part of a child's development and some aspects of teaching through adventure use play, but play and adventure are not the same thing. An adventure is a discrete experience often with a narrative structure of beginning, middle and end. An adventure includes uncertainty of outcome and there is always a link between the actions of the participants and the outcomes of the adventure.

Teaching through adventure is not about having thrills

There is a world of difference between having a thrill and having an adventure. A rollercoaster ride may be thrilling for children but they are merely passengers. Having an adventure is where children feel a sense of challenge, but have ownership and control of the experience and how they understand it. It is possible to have thrills in an adventure but this should not be the main point of the adventure, rather it might be an incidental feature or a planned high point.

Teaching through adventure is not about danger

Allowing children to have an adventure does not mean permitting uncontrolled risk taking, but it does require teachers to give children the opportunity to go through challenging experiences without being overprotected from the consequences of their actions. This requires teachers to plan the adventures carefully and ensure that any possible consequences are appropriate to the child. Rather than risk minimisation the teacher is responsible for a risk-benefit analysis and the child learns to judge and manage appropriate risk taking.

Teaching through adventure is not about visiting wild places

Wild places can provide a great location for adventures, but it is also possible to have an adventure in a familiar place. Although the location provides a backdrop to the adventure, it is transformed by the narrative and by the imagination of the child.

TEACHING THROUGH ADVENTURE: WHAT IT REALLY IS . . .

So what is teaching through adventure? We would argue that it is probably the most engaging form of teaching because it allows teachers to plan memorable activities relating to cognitive, affective and psychomotor learning and link these with children's innate love of the outdoors and their ability to imagine themselves into stories. Watching young people jump in muddy puddles or roll down a grassy hillside it is obvious that they are excited by the simplicity of the activity, the reality of the sensations and perhaps by the absence of artificial constraints, so that they feel a euphoric sense of connection to the place and activity. Similarly, when listening to children playing together it is clear that they enjoy putting themselves into imaginary situations and interacting with each other's creative ideas. They may be imagining themselves into stories that they already know and acting out existing roles within the structural constraints of the narrative, or they may be creating new stories and new roles. In both cases the narrative provides a framework for collaborative playing and interactive creativity and thus draws children with very different passions and interests into a single project. Thus, teaching through adventure uses real and memorable activities in the outdoors to fire children's creative imaginations and to facilitate collaborative working in order to support formal and informal learning.

An adventure is impactful. Children's play is quickly forgotten, but having an adventure is memorable. Even before setting out on an adventure, most children are engaged in imagining, worrying and dreaming about what will happen. During the adventure, the experience may feel intense and hyper-real to children as they have to learn new knowledge and skills, apply previous learning to real world situations and work together in unfamiliar ways. After the adventure children will often replay and narrate their adventures, using the experience to make links to classroom learning or as the basis for changes in behaviour or in their relationships with others. This intense and prolonged engagement with an adventure allows teachers to interweave educational and developmental objectives into the adventure to support child development and curriculum learning.

Adventures are often holistic experiences, introducing children to a range of different sensations, and creating connections between children; between children and adults; between children and the location and with the imagination. These connections may be novel and may challenge what a child feels comfortable with, but they add depth to the child's overall development. In particular, adventures may help children to explore their own yearning for risk and excitement. By connecting such yearnings to real experiences, children can understand their own needs for risk and excitement alongside an understanding of the difference between fantasy and reality. This pro-active engagement with the child's imagination helps to develop children into people who can differentiate between fantasy and reality.

Adventures always involve an element of risk-taking. This may be physical risk-taking, but might also involve children in the risk of failure or in taking emotional risks. By risk-taking (within limits controlled by the teacher) children develop an appreciation of the consequences of inappropriate risk-taking, but more importantly they can learn the value of trying new things and expanding their comfort zone. Outdoor activities that involve risk-taking are thus a way of preparing children to cope with the uncertainties that they will meet in later life. They provide a counter-balance to the tendency to over-protect children which can have the consequence of leaving children poorly prepared for life in an uncertain world. We feel that children need a regular dose of adventure outdoors to encourage them to experience and understand risk-taking through den building, camping, walking barefoot through the mud or toasting marshmallows on an open fire, or through more teacher-led activities such as orienteering and climbing.

Whilst adventures are often discrete, short-term experiences that form a relatively small part of a child's overall primary school experience, they are often highly memorable and remain with the individual long after other memories of school have faded. Thus there is likely to be an impact on the child's physical, social and cognitive development at the time of the adventure, but there is also the potential for impact when the individual recalls the adventure later in life.

Introducing adventure into primary school teaching can also have a school-wide impact. Angela Daniel, Head-teacher of Kingsland C of E Primary School in rural Herefordshire, is of the opinion that effective use of adventurous learning creates a school environment that enables children to feel 'secure enough to be vulnerable'. She feels that children are more willing to take risks, to undertake tasks where there is the possibility of failure, safe in the knowledge that should they fail they will be supported and praised by staff and their peers for taking that leap into the unknown. Maintaining a positive commitment to allowing children to take risks is often difficult for schools and there is considerable pressure on both teachers and schools to 'play safe' by selecting less ambitious plans or simply cutting the adventure out of their teaching. However the development of a school culture that recognises the value of vulnerability and openness to new adventures is very important to the development of the children and the ethos of the school. Finally, getting children involved in real-world adventures can wean children away from the sofa, mobile phones, social media and computer games, and encourage a passionate engagement with their environment and a healthy lifestyle. We believe that every teacher is capable of facilitating adventure for primary school children; after all if you take a group of young children into a woodland and leave them to it, they are more than capable of exploring, learning and entertaining themselves with little input from the accompanying adults. Thus the role of the teacher is not to enforce needless and overzealous constraints on the experience but to provide a scaffold for learning through adventure.

TEACHING THROUGH ADVENTURE: USING THE ADVENTURE WAVE

Whilst it would be enjoyable (and probably very popular) to simply plan the adventure around the creative ideas of the class, it is important to envisage adventure as part of the teaching plan and embed it within the learning outcomes for a particular topic. Particularly in larger schools the planning and coordination of learning activities is very important and teachers have limited flexibility, so there will inevitably be a compromise between

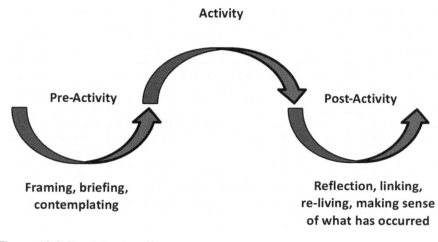

Figure 10.2 The Adventure Wave

(Image adapted from Panicucci 2007)

organisational requirements and the degree of independence given to the children. Similarly learning through adventure takes time, particularly when preparing children for the activity and reflecting on the activity afterwards. The process to support reflective learning within an adventure education experience is illustrated by the Adventure Wave (Schoel, Prouty & Radcliffe, 1988).

PLANNING AN ADVENTURE FOR CHILDREN

The pre-activity phase is really important as it starts to develop a narrative for the adventure. As the teacher, you will need to provide some information and guidance to frame the narrative within the topic, but also allow opportunities for the children to explore their own ideas of what will take place. This can be done verbally, through art, video or through engagement with other children's experiences. Children may at this stage become contemplative, worried, excited or all three and teachers must make judgements about how they support children particularly those who find unfamiliar activities stressful.

When introducing the activity the teacher should remember that the links to the topic are important as the eventual narrative needs to be anchored to the curriculum requirements, but that children should be free to overlay the topic with their own meanings and expectations. At this stage it is important to be clear with the children about the reasons for the activity, but to avoid giving your opinion on the meaning of the adventure. Similarly it is important to be clear about the likely content of the activity, but to avoid telling children what they will experience. Thus teachers can use a range of classroom and non-classroom activities to help the children to develop their ideas about the meaning of the adventure and to start to explore what they will experience during the adventure.

Alongside the learning activities, the pre-activity phase is an important time for preparation including gaining permission and consent as well as organising transport and any resources that may be needed. All this takes time and involves getting other people involved so it is important to get these underway early. As the procedures for educational visits vary between schools and across regions there is not sufficient space to provide guidance on planning – however, extensive advice and forms are available to teachers on the Outdoor Education Advisers' Panel website (www.oeap.info) and teachers should visit

---

ACTIVITY BOX

Creative task

Ask children to create a mask, shield or collage and decorate half with images of what they expect during their adventure. The other half is then decorated after the adventure as part of the reflection on change.

Narrative task

Ask children before, during or after their adventure to 'illustrate' each stage on a 'journey stick', by wrapping around different materials and weaving in various objects to tell the story and capture their adventure for retelling or future reference/review.

the *National Guidance for the Management of Outdoor Learning, off-site visits and learning outside the classroom* (available at http://oeap.info/what-we-do/oeap-guidance).

FACILITATING AN ADVENTURE FOR CHILDREN

The adventure belongs to the children, but the teacher has responsibility for making it happen in a safe and educative manner. If the planning and preparation have been done effectively then the teacher's role on the day is often as organiser and timekeeper; however this will vary with context and with the level of support. If the adventure requires technical skills and expertise or is in a remote or uncontrolled environment then the teacher and others may have to monitor children closely, but where possible children should be given freedom to approach the adventure in their own way. Within this, care should be taken to ensure that children are respectful of each other and that the approaches used include all children.

Where possible the facilitation should encourage and recognise creativity alongside mastery and personal development. This is not always possible at the time, so the teacher may need to collect artefacts, keep field notes or take photos of the experiences and the achievements of individuals.

PRACTICAL TIP

Always take a bag or a box so that children can bring back meaningful items – perhaps the twig that saved the world – and it can have pride of place in the classroom.

With some thought these can later be used to support classroom learning or to provide evidence of positive behaviour. Alternatively tasks can be designed to involve children in the development of their own evidence of learning.

PRACTICAL TASK

Provide a graphic map of the area or a list of skills that each child can use to set their own targets and to record their achievements.

Successful teaching through adventure is like any other teaching. Successful teachers are involved in supporting learning through planned activities and targeted inputs, but also have a responsibility to monitor and assess learning. If teachers find that they are too busy to watch the children then the activities will need to be amended to allow greater independence to the children. In order to do this it is useful to have a number of additional (low-risk) activities that can involve children in creative and imaginative tasks either individually or in small groups.

ACTIVITY BOX

Narrative task

Ask children to plan an imaginary journey across the landscape in front of them.

Creative task

Ask children to create a collage or picture of the landscape around them using the natural materials to hand.

Creative task

Ask children to observe and copy the movements of a living organism – a tree swaying, a woodlouse crawling, a bird hopping – and combine these into a small play or dance.

Creative task

Can they recreate the noises around them using natural materials – they can make a 'nature orchestra'.

It is important to remember that teaching through adventure is still teaching, and most of the approaches that work in a classroom will work in the adventurous venues. However the key difference is that the outdoors is full of sensory stimulation that can inspire creativity. The outdoors also provides opportunities for physical movement and imagination and the teacher is not constrained by four walls.

REFLECTING ON (AND LEARNING FROM) THE ADVENTURE

After the activity, time needs to be available for reflection, be it guided or self-motivated. Recalling the experience will allow children the opportunity to make sense of what has occurred, to link the learning back to the topic or to their earlier ideas, and to think about how they might do things differently in future. This reflection may be individual or shared and may take the form of art, drama, dance, poetry, creative writing or discussion. As with other topics, it is important to develop a progression and use a range of methods to reflect on the experience. A well-designed programme of reflection should move from recall and shallow reflection on what happened, to reflection on the meaning of the experience and on to the implications of the experience. This progression is often abbreviated to:

What? – So what? – Now what?

But why not use a more creative progression (Figure 10.4)?

Retell

Retelling an adventure converts a mixture of complicated and partially perceived experiences into a narrative. Activities can be as simple as allowing children to retell the

The jelly bean tree is one of many tools used by adventure/outdoor educators to initiate conversations with groups in order to review an activity or experience. One way of using the image is for children to identify a character that they think best suits their involvement and feelings regarding a recent activity or experience and explain their choice. Can you get a group of children to make their own natural 'jelly bean' tree for the group to stand on?

Figure 10.3 A jelly bean tree

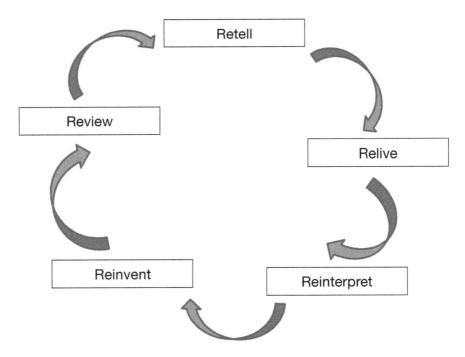

Figure 10.4 A creative progression

experience in small groups or could include activities such as creating a story board, a time line or a journey stick.

Relive

Whilst retelling can create narrative, acting out what happened, both the high and low points of the experience, can help children to explore experiences from a particular perspective. Including drama and acting can help children to explore actions and motivations, and can allow the teacher to focus on particular aspects of the learning.

Reinterpret

As children start to understand the experiences they move away from the simple narrative to something that starts to have layers of meaning. These can be simple metaphors such as hero quests or buddy stories, or might be about personal discovery or shared adventure. These can be explored in a range of creative ways, or might simply be revisiting the time line or story board to add text or images that reflect new understanding.

Reinvent

Reflection does not always need to be anchored to reality, and using inventive activities can be enjoyable and highly educative. Orienteering in a local park might provide links to classroom topics, but it also provides great opportunities for creativity. Art and drama projects or simple storytelling can be even more fun if the children feel free to invent animals, monsters and superheroes into the landscape or the activities or to reinvent the sequences, experiences and characters. The aim is not to overlay the learning experience with imaginary events, but to get the children to create alternatives where they can contextualise their experiences and explore different behaviours and outcomes.

Review

The reflective process needs to lead children to an understanding of their own learning so that they can apply this in future activities, and thus it may be useful for the reflective process to finish with children producing targets for themselves. This can be done as a whole class activity – possibly for presentation to the school – or as an individual task. When approached as an individual task, this is often done by asking children to write a letter to themselves to be opened in the future, or by writing a letter to parents/guardians. However there are many opportunities for creativity. Mask making or collage work can be used, or it might be fun to try a Haiku. As with all creative projects the teacher needs to set the parameters for the project and provide examples without limiting the authenticity of the artefacts.

CREATIVE TEACHING THROUGH ADVENTURE

Within the structure of teaching through adventure it is useful to keep in mind that this is not solely about curriculum delivery, but lies within child-centred learning. Thus there are three key questions that need to be foremost in teachers' minds when considering creative teaching through adventure. Why adventure? Whose adventure? And what adventure?

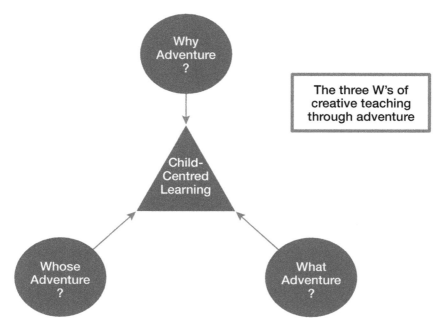

Figure 10.5 The three W's of creative teaching through adventure

Why adventure? Developing a creative narrative

An adventure needs an objective or needs to fit around a familiar narrative structure, although as children get older they feel more comfortable with undertaking adventures where the objectives are less clear. The teacher's role is to scaffold the experience, but not to take away the ownership or control.

The first creative act is to develop the objective and a supporting narrative. Initial teacher education often stresses the importance of planning learning activities, and in consequence many teachers see lesson planning as their own responsibility. However an adventure is a social construct. It is constructed around the imagination of the children and teachers. If a teacher can engage the children's imagination at an early stage then the narrative of the adventure will build through conversations and through play.

Whose adventure? Supporting the creative process

The role of the teacher within the adventure is that of facilitator, there to scaffold the experience, and as such to resist the temptation to influence the adventure's nature or outcome. The adventure belongs to the children, the teacher is there to support the thinking before and after the adventure, enabling the children to frame the adventure and reflect upon the experience. Strategies to do this might include art projects, classroom and small group discussions, drama or even interviewing older children about their experiences. This is one of the most enjoyable aspects of teaching through adventure as it requires the teacher to engage with the children's ideas and interweave them with curriculum and personal development aims within the constraints of feasibility.

What adventure? Choosing activities

There are a number of factors that will influence the choice of activities within the adventure and these will differ between schools and between groups. Broadly activities can be seen as sitting on a spectrum between hard adventure and soft adventure. At the hard adventure end of the spectrum are activities that require a high degree of technical competence to complete safely. At the soft adventure end are those that can be completed safely with less technical competence. In most cases there is a progression from soft adventure to more technical activities. The two case studies below show how a school has developed provision that is appropriate for children. The decision is less about how 'hard' an activity is, but more about how well it fits with the curriculum and the children's needs and whether there are opportunities within a reasonable distance.

CASE STUDY: KINGSLAND C OF E PRIMARY SCHOOL, HEREFORDSHIRE

Kingsland C of E Primary School is in the enviable position of having easy access to the rural environment, a year 5/6 teacher who trained as an outdoor education specialist and a supportive head teacher and governors. Adventures in the outdoors are viewed as an integral and essential element of pupils' education and school experience. The teaching staff highlight that experiences gained in the outdoors stay with their pupils and are always identified by the children as the highlights of their time at Kingsland. The year 5/6 teacher is of the opinion that exposing the pupils to adventures and the risks that accompany this encourages an 'honesty about self' that promotes independence, creative thinking and empathy once back in the more traditional classroom setting.

ACTIVITY BOX **CASE STUDY 1 – ORIENTEERING**

Orienteering is often seen as an easy option or 'a quick fix' for teachers with less experience in delivering outdoor adventures. Unfortunately if approached in this way orienteering is unlikely to inspire the children or the teachers. The following is a great example of how the year 5/6 teacher from Kingsland C of E Primary School used orienteering to develop a curriculum topic, to support personal development, to allow children to develop new skills and to give children a series of memorable adventures inside and outside the school grounds.

The children were introduced to maps as part of their 'mountains' topic. In order to understand about maps they drew sketch maps of the classroom. They progressed to drawing more accurate and detailed maps of the school grounds. After a class discussion these maps were used to run an initial orienteering event. The children were very enthusiastic about maps so the teacher arranged a visit to a nearby National Trust property to make use of their permanent orienteering course. Once there a small number of staff and helpers were dotted around the deciduous woodlands whilst the class teacher set the children off individually on a 'star' event. Each child was given the number of a location to visit. They used the map to decide where to go and then they ran into the woods to locate the point. On arrival at the marker, the child noted down the letters on the marker and returned to the teacher as fast as they could. On their return they were given the next point to visit.

▨ **Figure 10.6**
Teaching map
reading

(Photograph:
Kingsland C of E
primary school)

After returning to school, the children designed and delivered orienteering lessons to the children in Year 3 who had been introduced to maps through the Hundred Acre Wood pictorial map from the Winnie the Pooh stories. As a resource the older children were provided with the orienteering focused Outdoor Learning Cards (available from the OEAP). They used these to support the design of the orienteering lessons. The sessions were used to assess elements of the Junior Sports Leader Award that the children were working towards.

The sessions that the children designed and delivered allowed the older children to demonstrate their understanding of maps and to pass this on to the younger children. Later Year 3 children applied their skills on a visit to a local woodland where they navigated around a sculpture trail in small accompanied groups taking digital photos of the sculptures.

The Year 6 topic finished by scaling a real mountain, the Sugar Loaf. As this required additional support, the class teacher asked the course leader of an outdoor education degree at the University of Worcester if she could 'borrow' some suitably experienced and qualified students to support the trip. This rather cheeky request was well received and enabled small groups of children to use maps and compasses to navigate to the summit where they had lunch. Each group was accompanied by a student and a school member of staff, but the children made all of the decisions applying the knowledge and understanding developed within the topic to successfully climb the mountain.

The above teaching progression shows how the teacher structured the topic to provide the children with appropriate personal and shared challenges, the opportunity to develop mastery of new skills and to achieve a memorable success. These three elements are identified by McKenzie (2000) as aspects of learning that lead to personal growth.

It is also worth noting that the teachers brought in expertise from outside of the school. In this case it was a university, but schools could also access support through adventurous activity providers, FE colleges and through parent and teacher contacts. The use of external expertise requires careful planning and the approval of the head teacher, but can support teachers to provide high quality outdoor adventures, and provides a good example of working creatively within the outdoors.

ACTIVITY BOX **CASE STUDY 2 – CLIMBING**

Rock climbing might appear to be beyond the reach of primary schools, but approached with imagination and, if necessary, calling on external support it can be as achievable as running orienteering within the school grounds.

Climbing in schools has undergone a renaissance in the past few years with increasing numbers of primary schools visiting climbing venues. Bouldering, climbing without the use of ropes, is becoming more common, with traversing walls and low level bouldering walls appearing in many playgrounds and sports halls. The number of climbing walls in the UK is also on the rise meaning that most schools have reasonable access to indoor climbing venues.

As with the earlier orienteering example, any activity undertaken as an educational experience, rather than as a recreational activity, should provide children with the opportunity to develop mastery of new skills and a greater appreciation of themselves, others and the world around them. The following is an example of a clearly structured and imaginative climbing session.

Having gained a grant for developing new sporting activities within their school, the teaching team decided that a traversing wall in the playground would provide children with the opportunity for independent, adventurous play during break times. Such was

■ **Figure 10.7**
Primary school children and supervised climbing

the popularity of the wall that staff started to incorporate the bouldering-specific activities found in the Outdoor Learning Cards into their PE lessons, focusing on movement skills and peer support. Improvements in climbing ability were clear within a very short period of time and the teaching team felt that more adventurous climbing based activities would be the next logical step. With some free local expert assistance a number of suitable mature trees within the school grounds were identified as being 'climbable'. The trees were used to introduce the children to climbing harnesses, ropes, knots and the belay devices necessary to safeguard each other whilst climbing. The tree climbing increased the perceived level of adventure, introduced new skills to be mastered and engendered trust between peers. Such was the success of tree climbing that the school arranged a day at a nearby outdoor climbing venue, Symonds Yat in the Wye Valley. The aim of the day was for the children, under supervision, to deliver a day of climbing for a group of their peers from a nearby cluster school with whom they would be attending secondary school in the autumn term.

The day was very successful with children from both schools enjoying the opportunity to develop new skills, make new friends and take responsibility for other people. The outcomes of the day were reviewed by staff and children at both schools and the teachers framed class discussions and reflective tasks around preparation for the move to secondary school.

Since then, climbing in the school has gone from strength to strength with the development of an after-school climbing club using a local indoor wall, and has provided a wider range of opportunities for children. As the Head Teacher says 'the inclusion of new activities that are less mainstream has enabled those children who aren't interested in football or netball to shine and the positive impact this has had on their standing in the peer group, self-confidence and self-esteem has been immeasurable'. In part this has been because climbing has been embedded within a reflective model of learning. Children have been encouraged to reflect on their development of climbing skill and interpersonal skills at the end of each session, encouraged to be critical of their own performance and to identify ways in which to improve. The year 5/6 teacher is of the opinion that this reflective practice is now filtering in to the academic work produced by the children and is having a positive impact on their approach and the quality of work produced.

In this case, the safe development of climbing required equipment, qualifications and expertise that was not available in the school. The school employed some professional support, but most of the qualifications and expertise were available through parents, governors and personal contacts. Where this is not available, schools could approach adventurous activity providers or collaborate with other schools. Where schools wish to develop this area further it may be sensible to support teaching staff to gain the Climbing Wall Award (CWA) which allows holders to supervise bouldering and climbing wall activities, or Single Pitch Award (SPA) for outdoor climbing sessions. These qualifications are available from Mountain Training, the body responsible for UK based climbing and mountaineering qualifications (www.mountain-training.org). Teachers might also consider award schemes such as the National Indoor Climbing Award Scheme (NICAS). This has 5 levels from Foundation Climber (level 1) to Advanced Climber (Level 5) and Levels 1 and 2 are particularly suitable for primary school children. NICAS has been likened to swimming badges for climbers, with badges and certificates awarded as each level is completed (www.nicas.co.uk).

FINAL WORDS

We hope that this chapter has introduced teachers to the more adventurous side of teaching outdoors and examined the opportunities to create and support children's adventures on or off the school grounds. The case studies from a rural primary school show how outdoor adventures can become a normal part of primary school education, and that teachers can use their teaching skills (augmented where necessary by practical skills) to provide a wider and more imaginative curriculum.

If we were to have one *take-home message* for this chapter it would be to say that in the same way that teacher trainees find that it takes time to adapt to teaching in a classroom, so it also takes time to become comfortable teaching outdoors. However it is worth the effort: there are wonderful opportunities for curriculum enhancement from taking learning out of the classroom; children who may not shine in a classroom suddenly demonstrate skills and abilities that were hidden; children develop passions that bring excitement to their school life; and children build memories that last a lifetime. In addition the outdoors stimulates and energises project-based teaching, as teachers find they have access to a whole new palate of creative tasks that makes teaching both rewarding and effective.

ACKNOWLEDGEMENT

All images are courtesy of the authors and Kingsland C of E Primary School.

BIBLIOGRAPHY

Ball, D., Gill, T. and Spiegal, B. (2008) *Managing Risk in Play Provision: Implementation Guide*. Penrith, English Outdoor Council.

Barrett, J. and Greenaway, R. (1995) *Why Adventure? The Role and Value of Outdoor Adventure in Young People's Personal and Social Development: A Review of Research*. Coventry, The Foundation for Outdoor Adventure.

Barton, B. (2006) *Safety, Risk and Adventure in Outdoor Activities*. London, Sage Publications.

Beames, S., Higgins, P. and Nicol, R. (2012) *Learning Outside the Classroom: Theory and Guidelines for Practice*. London, Routledge.

Beard, C. L and Wilson, J. P. (2013) *Experiential Learning: A Handbook for Education, Training and Coaching*. London, Kogan Page Publishers.

Berry, M. and Hodgson, C. (2011) *Adventure Education: An Introduction*. London, Routledge.

Christie, B., Higgins, P. and McLaughlin, P. (2014) 'Did you enjoy your holiday?' Can residential outdoor learning benefit mainstream schooling? *Journal of Adventure Education & Outdoor Learning*, 14(1), 1–23.

Cooper, G. (1998) *Outdoors with Young People*. Lyme Regis, Russell House Publishing.

Davis, B., Rea, T. and Waite, S. (2006) The special nature of the outdoors: its contribution to the education of children aged 3–11. *Australian Journal of Outdoor Education*, 10(2), 3.

Ewert, A. W., Sibthorp, R. J. and Sibthorp, J. (2014) *Outdoor Adventure Education: Foundations, Theory, and Research*. USA, Human Kinetics.

Gilbertson, K., Bates, T., McLaughlin, T. and Ewert, A. (2006) *Outdoor Education: Methods and Strategies*. USA, Human Kinetics.

Gill, T. (2010) *Nothing Ventured: Balancing Risks and Benefits in the Outdoors*. Penrith, English Outdoor Council.

Gill, T. (2015) *High Quality Outdoor Learning*. Penrith, English Outdoor Council.

Humberstone, B. and Stan, I. (2011) Outdoor learning: primary pupils' experiences and teachers' interaction in outdoor learning. *Education 3–13*, 39(5), 529–540.

McKenzie, M.D. (2000) How are adventure education program outcomes achieved? A review of the literature. *Australian Journal of Outdoor Education,* 5(1), 19–28.

Mortlock, C. (1987) *The Adventure Alternative*. Cumbria, Cicerone Press Limited.

Mygind, E. (2009) A comparison of childrens' statements about social relations and teaching in the classroom and in the outdoor environment. *Journal of Adventure Education & Outdoor Learning*, 9(2), 151–169.

Outdoor Education Advisers' Panel and English Outdoor Council (2015*) High Quality Outdoor Learning* (Rev. edn). U.K., English Outdoor Council.

Outdoor Education Advisers' Panel (2014) *National Guidance for the Management of Outdoor Learning, Off-site Visits and Learning Outside the Classroom*. Available at: http://oeap. info/what-we-do/oeap-guidance (accessed 15 January 2016).

Panicucci, J. (2007) Cornerstones of adventure education. In Prouty, D., Panicucci, J. and Collinson, R. (2007) *Adventure Education Theory and Applications*. Champaign, IL, Human Kinetics, pp. 33–48.

Pether, T. (2012) *Leadership for Embedding Outdoor Learning Within the Primary Curriculum*. Nottingham, National College for School Leadership.

Pickard, A. and Maude, P. (2014) *Teaching Physical Education Creatively*. London, Routledge.

Rea, T. (2008) Alternative visions of learning: children's learning experiences in the outdoors. *Educational Futures*, 1(2), 42–50.

Robertson, J. (2014) *Dirty Teaching: A Beginner's Guide to Learning Outdoors*. Carmarthen, Independent Thinking Press.

Schoel, J., Prouty, D. and Radcliffe, P. (1988) *Islands of Healing: A Guide to Adventure Based Counselling*. Hamilton, MA, Project Adventure.

Solly, K. S. (2014) *Risk, Challenge and Adventure in the Early Years: A Practical Guide to Exploring and Extending Learning Outdoors*. London, Routledge.

Swarbrooke, J., Beard, C., Leckie, S. and Pomfret, G. (2003) *Adventure Tourism: The New Frontier*. London, Routledge.

Waite, S. (2007) 'Memories are made of this': some reflections on outdoor learning and recall. *Education 3–13*, 35(4), 333–347.

Waite, S. (2010) Losing our way? The downward path for outdoor learning for children aged 2–11 years. *Journal of Adventure Education & Outdoor Learning*, 10(2), 111–126.

Waite, S. (2011) Teaching and learning outside the classroom: personal values, alternative pedagogies and standards. *Education 3–13*, 39(1), 65–82.

Waite, S., Huggins, V. and Wickett, K. (2014) Risky outdoor play: embracing uncertainty in pursuit of learning. *Outdoor Play in the Early Years*, 71–85.

THE FUTURE OUTDOORS

Learning from around the world

Stephen Pickering

PEERING INTO THE FUTURE

For many young people the educational landscape is one in which 'societal inequalities are played out and reproduced rather than overcome' (Gillies, 2008, in Carroll and McCullogh, 2014, p.4). The issue is that within societies greater value seems to be placed on the publication of statistics to demonstrate learning rather than on the value of learning itself. Learning outdoors bucks the trend in that the emphasis sits squarely on the intrinsic beauty of learning for learning's sake. The results are perhaps less tangible than those from a test but are no less powerful. So how do we raise our voice against the current educational philosophy that seems to demand test scores as a means to measure success?

Our own personal educational values – and the educational values of society – are shaped by our experiences, by previous philosophies and philosophers and by current trends (Gray and Macblain, 2015). Perhaps it is time to peer into the murky world of the future, for surely that is the world that children and schools will soon inhabit. We may not be able to predict the future; however, I believe that we can influence it. History has provided us with many examples of culture followed by anti-culture. I wonder if the increased usage of technology in schools and society will soon lead to a kick-back against such screen-important worlds and re-engagement with the natural world. Indeed, I think this counter-revolution has already started. There are some important questions to answer here. Firstly, can outdoor learning sit comfortably as a natural and important part of children's development, learning and upbringing within a society where the natural world is steadily being replaced by the man-made? And secondly, can a focus on outdoor learning with young children help to provide the impetus, skills and motivation to preserve, conserve and expand our vital natural environments?

For many children, outdoor learning entails stepping through the classroom door into an outdoor area, be that natural or largely man-made. This doorway creates a 'perceptual boundary' (Warden, 2015) almost like the Narnia wardrobe. And whilst it is super to have something exciting to look forward to – 'It's Welly Wednesday!' – the fact that learning outside is seen by many as a treat, as something special to look forward to, does not necessarily help learning outside to be normal working in the way that being in the classroom is seen to be. Perhaps we should turn things around a little; take the register, assemblies, notices or indeed learning outside: make going inside the treat and normalise outdoor learning.

HOW TO SIT OUTDOORS

Twenty-five years ago I was lucky enough to embark on a wonderful adventure, spending ten days with a group of indigenous people who lived in the Ecuadorian Amazon. It is interesting from an educational perspective to note that I remember those ten days better than most others in my life. The people were Amazonian Indians, although not in the sense that you are probably dreaming of right now. There were no amazing piercings and jewellery, no shrunken heads hanging in their homes. They wore shorts and T-shirts and they lived absolutely at one with nature. They bought products from the market (a day's boat ride away) and their children attended school (allegedly). But they lived with the forest around them, eating what they caught and collected. I was amazed by much of what I saw, but a very commonplace thing really struck me. There were no chairs. They would just sit on their haunches, feet flat on the ground. It was brilliant as they could do that anywhere. Why have a chair if you don't need one! I tried to copy them and really struggled, for it was as if I were built differently. However, by the end of ten days I could sit as they did, quite comfortably, and for a reasonable amount of time. I was so pleased with myself! I was learning from those who really knew. On reflection, this simple lesson was important to me and now I believe that we need to look towards those who know how to live successfully in our natural world when we consider the future. A successful society is not necessarily a materially rich one (although it can be), but it is one where the people live well and provide for future generations. I think we need to look at the societies and cultures whose outdoor lives have continued successfully for hundreds, perhaps thousands of years. And so for this final chapter I have looked to case studies from around the world.

FRILUFTSLIV

The Norwegian tradition of friluftsliv basically means being free with nature. Norway is a sparsely populated country with a dramatic and quite unique North European landscape created over millennia by successions of ice ages and the mixed processes of ice and ocean battering the coastline. Being a long, narrow country, the coastline forms a major part of Norwegian topography. Friluftsliv is predicated on the right of public access (Sandell, 2007) whereby (with a few restrictions like land that is currently cultivated and respect for homes and other groups of people) everyone can roam wherever they like over the land and can pitch their tent anywhere, too. Friluftsliv works well, not just in Norway, but in other North European countries too, based on the inculcation and education of respect for people and the landscape. It would be easy to think of friluftsliv as being for young, intrepid and adventurous people, but rather than being seen as adventure into the wilderness, allemansträtt (which means the right of public access to the countryside) is seen as 'more of a cultural landscape' (Sandell, 2007) used regularly by families and wide ranging groups of people, often just in the evenings after work or at weekends as a regular practice rather than as a major excursion. Loynes (2007) is vociferous in his argument against the corporate outdoor activities like mountain biking, bungee jumping and ropes courses, describing how these neglect the true values of free and easy experiences with nature in favour of 'a marketable commodity' (Loynes, 2007). The parallel arguments are easy to see in a British primary education context with adventure holidays and canoeing trips, PE lessons and orienteering pitched against Forest Schools and woodland walks. My view is that the methods by which we help and provide opportunities for children to engage in, and learn from, our natural world should be as wide and as varied as children are themselves. Loynes's argument of the power and importance of the development of values through friluftsliv is a strong one. He talks about values that relate to the landscape and its preservation in a time of environmental injustice. In some ways this equates to the value of walking with the class. We can probably all think of examples when a walk with your class has provided an opportunity for you to get to know some of your children in different and positive ways. A simple walk provides the space and opportunity for children to talk about the things that are important to them, so when you next go on a walk with your class leave the worksheets and the 'things to look out for . . .' behind and let the children's thoughts and motivations take over. I also believe the development of personal values, self-fulfilment and overcoming challenge that a child can achieve by succeeding through the more 'corporate' means like a difficult ropes course, for example, are important, too. Figure 11.1 is an attempt to portray this divide diagrammatically. The question that this raises for teachers is 'at which point within this diagram would you place the outdoor activities that you create and manage for your children? Is there a way to ensure a balance between personal experience and an 'eco-relationship' (Henderson, 2007)? Perhaps there needs to be greater connection between providers of outdoor education and the schools that make use of them. If schools can connect with their local providers so that they can say what they want in terms of learning and the National Curriculum then provision can focus on individual schools' needs and a balance can be found for future provision.

ACTIVITY BOX

As a teacher can you plot a range of activities for your children to ensure a balance between a) respect and appreciation for the outdoor environment and b) personal challenge and experience? Two examples are given in Figure 11.1. Where would you place your school's Forest School experience, PE lessons, orienteering, rock climbing, nature walks, canoeing, residential trips, field trips, or other experiences, on this figure? How do you feel the children may view the outdoors as a result of the activities they engage in when in school?

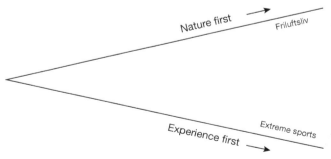

■ **Figure 11.1** The relationship between personal experience and an eco-relationship

THE TUAREG

The Tuareg are traditionally a nomadic Saharan cultural group of people, similar to but distinct from the Berbers of Algeria. They live off and live with one of the harshest environments on Earth and over thousands of years have developed a deep respect for and understanding of the world around them. Because the environment is so huge and so harsh they live within the culture of the landscape – a way of living which is markedly different from our modern Western world, which has shaped and managed the environment to suit our changing culture. So what can we possibly learn from such a group of people? Well clearly respect, the importance of knowledge and the ability to live with the elements, but I want to focus on one word: assouf, from the ancient Tamashek language. Assouf can mean many things; perhaps because our environment is so different it is difficult for us to find a simple translation. Assouf has been described as 'everything which lies out there in the darkness, beyond the warmth of the campfire' (unspecified Tuareg source). What a beautiful, magical word!

Our children are filled with imagination; and woodlands, meadows and fields are full of a spiritual essence: a sense of adventure: a sense of assouf! Wouldn't it be wonderful to provide the opportunity for our children to experience assouf: to be able to sit in a woodland clearing and revel in the hugeness of the world waiting there just behind them. Just imagine the creative work that could develop from such thinking and imagination. Slow pedagogy (Payne and Wattchow, 2009) provides space and time for children to stop, think and absorb the world around them. To have a class stand in a circle, backs to each other, with eyes shut and ask them just to listen is a magical experience. Or perhaps if you are at a Forest School setting get the children to face out when sitting round the fire rather than face in, shut their eyes and imagine the world beyond them: the first few metres, the next few miles and then across the country, past towns and out into the World. Assouf can be different things to different people. Another idea is for children to stand still and (without looking up) imagine what the space above them looks like. Ask the children to focus on the colours and shapes that may be above their heads – and then let the children look up and compare the real world with their imagined one. Or next time the children spot a bird flying overhead, stop the children and give them time to pause and imagine what the bird may be seeing, or what the bird will be thinking even. Assouf is all about imagination from a different perspective. There are many examples in the classroom when we require children to write from different perspectives, or to construct arguments from different points of view. Goswami (2008, 2015) describes how learning becomes more secure if children are given the opportunity to transfer thinking between different contexts. Assouf is a great way to start. Once children understand that they can see things from different perspectives and that there are views other than their own which they can access with a little imagination, then that skill can be applied to written work, class debates and many other activities.

JAPAN

In Japan the historical, cultural and spiritual landscape is viewed as an integral part of the natural world with three types of cultural landscapes identified (Ishida, 2005, cited in Kameoka, 2009). These are: the man-made landscapes, and we are all aware of the beautiful and spiritually designed Japanese gardens; the cultural landscapes formed by human activities like farming, and again awe-inspiring rice terraces scaling dizzying hillsides are a well-known feature; and landscapes associated with religion and arts, such as mountains blessed by spirits, sacred trees and an environment intertwined with story. Huudo is the Japanese name given to the relationship between a community and the environment of which it is a part (Kameoka, 2009). There is seen to be a timeless co-existing balance between the community and nature and for each community the geography, history and climate can create 'different types of socio-environmental relationships' (Kameoka, 2009, p.3). Minakata categorises these relationships as being ecology of biology, ecology of society and ecology of mind (Minakata, 1867–1941, in Kameoka, 2009). This notion of your local environment being rich in history and stories from the past – of myths that could have taken place just beyond the school grounds – is a wonderful place from which to develop art and literature with children whilst helping them to feel a true sense of place in their locale. Local geographical and historical knowledge is not just about facts, but also the layering of stories (Brookes, 2002), and this can provide a route for children to engage in understanding their own place in society and in nature. We can each weave our own stories around the places we value. There are two different aspects of affective learning (Roberts 1992; Pearlman Hougie, 2010). Firstly there is the notion of an emotion or feeling attached to an object or place. Children grow very fond of their Forest School site, for example, and many have favourite places in the school fields and playgrounds. Children attach a value to many of the places they visit and experience. The second notion is that these feelings and emotions can influence their attitudes and values. I have witnessed children who have previously demonstrated a fear of insects like flies, wasps and spiders in the classroom, taking time to watch and even care for the very same species out on the Forest School site. The hope is that this more positive and caring view towards animals found in nature will lead to a more positive attitude towards creatures generally. Taking children out on a regular basis to local environments can help children to develop this 'socio-environmental relationship'. As the children learn about their local area and environment both affectively and cognitively they also learn about themselves and perhaps help to foster this balance between nature and society.

CANADA

The province of Ontario took a radical step with their education provision by posing the question, 'what should students know, do and value by the time they graduate from school?' (Hopkins, 2016). After a long consultation process with students, parents, businesses and community groups an outcomes-based curriculum was devised based on six key outcomes for graduating students (Box 11.1). Hopkins, writing as chair of a UNESCO report, points out how interesting it is to note that sustainability in a broad sense is reflected throughout the six outcome statements (UNESCO, 2005).

Canada scores very well in the OECD league tables for education, appearing in or near the top ten and consistently above the UK in English, Maths and Science (*The Telegraph*, 2016), so the curriculum set out above is one that works. The curriculum set out above can be viewed as a challenge to other curricula around the world. It is a view of teaching and learning where education is based on processes of learning and the development of values. Additionally it is a curriculum where the state of the environment and sustainable practices for future growth and development are highlighted as a focus. Our latest National Curriculum for England in primary schools (DFE, 2013) has been deliberately slimmed

ACTIVITY BOX **AN INTERVIEW WITH A TREE**

I had been working with some children at a local nature reserve and we discovered that the nature reserve had once been the site of a World War I hospital. In fact the path that we had used each week, looking out for rabbits as we walked down the Forest School site, had been known as Matron's walk, as it used to lead around the edge of the main ward buildings. Some of the trees may well have been there when the hospital was full of soldiers and because there were no soldiers left around we decided to interview the trees to find out what they had seen over the years! Interviewing trees is a fantastic way to give purpose to imagination. The first part of the exercise is for the children to think of the questions they would like to ask the tree. I wanted a focus on the history of the place, but the children could ask anything and so the questions ranged from 'who was your favourite wounded soldier?' to 'do squirrels tickle?' Thinking up the questions is a great activity by itself, but we all know that the trees can't answer, even if they listened carefully and really wanted to, so the next stage was to put children in pairs with one standing in front of the tree to ask questions and the other to stand behind the tree and answer on behalf of the tree.

Now it does not take much to imagine the joy and fun that ensued from such an activity. The children loved hiding behind trees and putting on suitable 'tree voices'. But in addition to the fun there was a huge amount of creative, imaginative learning. The children were thinking from different perspectives, they were engaging with history, the spirit of the woodland and using purposeful imagination.

I would like to take this idea further. Trees have long been regarded as being wise; guardians of our countryside even. Many children may know about the Elts – or wise trees of Tolkein's world. What advice might trees provide for our future? Rather than focus questions on the past why not encourage children to ask the trees questions about the future? What would you like the future to be? What might happen if you were cut down? What might happen if all the trees were cut down? Children will be asked to consider notions of sustainability, and by answering the questions they are being asked to consider the future. It is hoped that the answers given by the children hiding behind and representing the trees might provide positive solutions for a sustainable future. And why stop with trees, if you want to really challenge some creative children, ask them to interview a stone. After all, the stone they choose will have been formed millions of years ago!

■ **Figure 11.2** Interviewing a tree

(Photo Stephen Pickering)

BOX 11.1 THE SIX KEY OUTCOMES OF THE TORONTO OUTCOMES-BASED CURRICULUM

Literacy

With literacy emphasis was placed on using literacy in order to solve problems, engage in debate and think critically. In other words, the development of literacy was to have a clear purpose based on creative skills.

Aesthetic appreciation and creativity

It is really interesting to see aesthetic appreciation of both natural and human environments being placed as one of six key outcomes. Added to this is a call for students to 'participate in creative activity and expression' (Hopkins, 2016).

Communication and collaboration

Many curricula around the world have a strong emphasis on effective communication, but fewer emphasise collaborative skills as an outcome to acquire. There is a real sense that the Toronto curriculum has a context of mutual understanding and respect.

Information management

The key point for me here is the statement made that the huge array of information resources currently available are used 'to make sound decisions and to take responsible actions' (Hopkins, 2016).

Responsible citizenship

And I quote: 'Our students will value the diversity of the world's people, cultures, and eco-systems. They will understand and actively promote equity, justice, peace, the democratic process, and the protection of the environment in their own community, Canada, and the world' (Hopkins, 2016).

Personal life skills, values and actions

The emphasis with this last outcome is based on a notion of active care: care for themselves and others and for the environment around them.

down in many areas, particularly within foundation subjects, so that schools have freedom to deliver the National Curriculum as one vital part of their School Curriculum:

> 2.1 Every state-funded school must offer a curriculum which is balanced and broadly based and which: promotes the spiritual, moral, cultural, mental and physical development of pupils at the school and of society, and prepares pupils at the school for the opportunities, responsibilities and experiences of later life.

> 2.2 The school curriculum comprises all learning and other experiences that each school plans for its pupils. The national curriculum forms one part of the school curriculum.

> (DFE, 2013, p.5)

ACTIVITY BOX **THE FIVE R'S**

Sustainability can be a confusing idea for children and is often misinterpreted as simply turning off lights and recycling paper. The Five R's of sustainability can be used to help children view the breadth of sustainability. Many lesson ideas can be derived from each of the five R's. A litter survey in the local area can raise questions of unnecessary waste. Can children create artwork using waste found? Can they re-design packaging that uses fewer materials (Easter eggs are good examples to use here)? Can natural materials found outside be used to create objects that are usually made of man-made materials like plastic? These lesson examples can often form a bridge between learning outside and inside. I like to use the hand shown in Figure 11.3 to demonstrate the Five R's of sustainability because it is easy for the children to see how Respect, being the thumb, can easily connect to each of the other R's. Pickering suggests an activity entitled 'Does our school care' (Pickering, 2013, p.177) where children complete a sustainability enquiry of their school environment using the term 'care' as a vehicle to help young children understand sustainability.

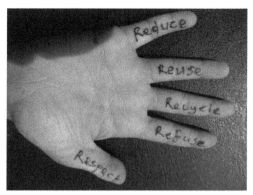

▨ **Figure 11.3** The Five R's of sustainability

(Photo Stephen Pickering)

Each of those six noted outcomes above (literacy, aesthetic appreciation and creativity, communication and collaboration, information management, responsible citizenship and personal life skills, values and actions) can easily be found within examples of creative teaching and learning outdoors that take place up and down our country on a daily basis. Teachers in the UK have the opportunity to develop creative teaching outdoors, that encompasses the excellent practice seen in Toronto and other places, within their own curriculum framework. Indeed if one adopts a sustainable futures philosophy of 'living today with tomorrow in mind', then perhaps we have a responsibility to do so.

CREATIVITY AND CRITICAL THINKING

Consider for a moment, if you will, a pride of lions out on the Serengeti plains. Dad will be lounging, seemingly unconcerned under a tree, surrounded by a more diligent harem of lionesses. The lion cubs, meanwhile, scamper and play around, rising up to each other in mock battles. Mum will be trying to get a well-earned rest but the cubs clamber up her and then leap off with an attempt at a growl to pounce on an unsuspecting beetle. Yes, it is abundantly clear that animals learn through play. The adults keep their offspring safe, they provide food and shelter and they even model correct behaviour, but they basically allow their cubs to learn by trial and error. And the cubs want to learn.

We, however, live in a more complex society. We can't lounge under trees because we have to go to work, so teachers do the job of teaching the children to live in the World. But then of course the teachers need to be regulated because it is a 'big thing' to leave your children in someone else's care. And this is where the issues with education today start. Teachers have to teach. Of course they do, and teachers are brilliant. Teachers are dedicated, conscientious and skilled. They do not have the luxury of having just four cubs to look out for. They have thirty. They also mainly teach children within the four walls of the classroom. And these restrictions bring many benefits, but they also bring limitations. Teachers work hard to deliver individualised, differentiated learning because it is clear that different children learn differently. But when it comes to behaviour, by and large, conformity becomes an important vehicle. Behaviourist rewards and sanctions, through the bribery of treats coupled with the threat of punishment, or zone boards somewhat like medieval depictions of heaven and hell, became the staple of the classroom. We accept that play is a vital element of learning. Behaviour is too. Behaviour and play are inextricably linked. It is through play – amongst many other things – that children learn behaviour skills. And yet, whilst in the classroom we differentiate to accommodate children's different learning styles it is far more difficult to differentiate for children's different behaviour styles. And this happens for very good reasons, too. When you take the children outside the need for conformity tends to dissipate (although there are clear behaviour guidelines and rules to ensure safety). This is not to say that we do not need rules to maintain good, safe learning outside, but behaviour management techniques seem to change and children are generally allowed to behave more naturally. And this freedom allows children to let their imagination flourish which in turn leads to purposeful play and purposeful learning. If creativity is accepted as purposeful imagination then critical thinking is the internal process that children go through to turn the imagination into creative learning. The Forest School ethos, to cite just one of many excellent vehicles for learning outdoors, is very firmly rooted in self-discovery with the teacher as a facilitator of the children's learning. Or to put it another way the teachers stand back and let 'the children get on with the business of learning' (Kelly and Cutting, 2011, p. 107). Padget (2013) describes how teaching has changed over the years to a model based on facilitation rather than dictation through a better and emerging understanding of how children learn and a motivation for teachers to help children to develop critical thinking skills. Warden (2015) poses an important question: when teaching outdoors are we really looking, in a constructivist sense, to develop new knowledge? Are we, in effect, simply teachers working in a different environment to the classroom, or are we in fact encouraging the children to engage in activities and discovery of their own that may lead to a shift and a development in thinking? I suppose the answer lies in the paradox of education: is our education system designed to enable learners to learn how to learn or is it there for us to teach children the things we think they need to know? This is very simplistic as clearly there is a necessary balance between the two, but perhaps learning outdoors provides a vital vehicle for children to develop critical thinking skills within an environment that is markedly different from the classroom in terms of structure and often pedagogies, too. The key to creative teaching outdoors is for us to be able to provide the opportunities for the children to develop critical thinking and purposeful learning outdoors, and then to enable and encourage the application of these skills and values in other situations, including back in the classroom.

REFERENCES

Brookes, A. (2002) Gilbert White never came this far South: Naturalist knowledge and the limits of universalist environmental education. *Canadian Journal of Environmental Education*, 7(2), 73–87.

Carroll, M. and McCullogh, M. (eds) (2014) *Understanding Teaching and Learning in Primary Education.* London, Sage.

DFE (2013) *The National Curriculum in England Key Stages 1 and 2 Framework Document.* London, DFE.

Goswami, U. (2008) Principles of learning, implications for teaching: a cognitive neuroscience perspective. *Journal of Philosophy of Education*, 42, 3–4.

Goswami, U. (2015) *Children's Cognitive Development And Learning CPRT Research Survey 3 (new series).* Cambridge Primary Review Trust. Cambridge, Pearson.

Gray, C. and MacBlain, S. (2015) (2nd edn) *Learning Theories in Childhood.* London, Sage.

Henderson, B. (2007) Introduction: a Canadian meets friluftsliv. In Henderson, B. and Vikander, N. (eds) *Nature First. Outdoor Life the Friluftsliv Way.* Toronto, Natural Heritage Books.

Hopkins, C.A (2016) *Toronto Board of Education Curriculum Revision and Reorientation.* Available at: www.esdtoolkit.org/discussion/case_study.htm (accessed June 2016).

Kameoka, Y. (2009) *Cultural Dimensions of Outdoor Education in Mt Koya, Japan: Co-existing Patterns of Universalist and Local Outdoor Education Approaches.* La Trobe University, Bendigo.

Kelly, O. and Cutting, R. (2011) Understanding places and society through history and geography outside the classroom. In Waite, S. (ed.) *Children Learning Outside the Classroom From Birth to Eleven.* London, Sage.

Loynes, C. (2007) Why outdoor learning should get real. In Henderson, B. and Vikander, N. *Nature First. Outdoor Life the Friluftsliv Way.* Toronto: Natural Heritage Books.

Padget, S. (2013) *Creativity and Critical Thinking. Teaching Contemporary Themes in Secondary Education.* London, David Fulton, Routledge.

Payne, P.G. and Wattchow, B. (2009) Phenomenological deconstruction, slow pedagogy, and the corporeal turn in wild environmental/outdoor education. *Canadian Journal of Environmental Education*, 14, 15–32.

Pearlman Hougie, D. (2010) Learning outside the comfort zone. *Primary Geography,* 73, 26–27.

Pickering, S. (2013) Keeping geography messy. In Scoffham, S. (ed.) *Teaching Geography Creatively.* London, Routledge.

Roberts, l. (1992) Affective learning, affective experience: what does it have to do with museum education? In Benehold, A., Bitgood, S. and Shettel, H. (eds) *Visitor Studies: Theory, Research and Practice,* volume 4. Jacksonville, AL: Center for Social Design.

Sandell, K. (2007) The right of public access: the landscape perspective of friluftsliv. In Henderson, B. and Vikander, N. (eds) (2007) *Nature First. Outdoor Life the Friluftsliv Way.* Toronto, Natural Heritage Books.

The Telegraph (2016) OECD Education Report. Available at: www.telegraph.co.uk/education/leaguetables/10488555/OECD-education-report-subject-results-in-full.html (accessed June 2016).

UNESCO (2005) *Guidelines and Recommendations for Reorienting Teacher Education to Address Sustainability.* Education for sustainable development in action. Technical Paper No. 2.

Warden, C. (2015) *Learning with Nature. Embedding Outdoor Practice.* London, Sage.

INDEX